Aberdeenshire

COUNCIL

Aberdeenshire Library and Information Service
www.aberdeenshire.gov.uk/libraries
Renewals Hotline 01224 661511

NORMANDY

★ Best places

-164

3025844

Original text by Nia Williams

Updated by Nia Williams

ISBN 978-0-7495-6677-7

Published by AA Publishing, a trading name of AA Media Limited, whose registered office is Fanum House, Basing View, Basingstoke, Hampshire RG21 4EA. Registered number 06112600.

A CIP catalogue record for this book is available from the British Library

Colour separation: MRM Graphics Ltd
Printed and bound in Italy by Printer Trento S.r.l.

A04192
Maps in this title produced from mapping © MAIRDUMONT / Falk Verlag 2010 with updates from mapping © ISTITUTO GEOGRAFICO DE AGOSTINI S.P.A., NOVARA 2007
Transport map © Communicarta Ltd, UK

About this book

Symbols are used to denote the following categories:

➕ map reference to maps on cover

✉ address or location

☎ telephone number

🕐 opening times

💷 admission charge

🍽 restaurant or café on premises
or nearby

Ⓜ nearest underground train station

🚌 nearest bus/tram route

🚊 nearest overground train station

⛴ nearest ferry stop

✈ nearest airport

❓ other practical information

ℹ tourist information office

➤ indicates the page where you will
find a fuller description

This book is divided into five sections.

The essence of Normandy pages 6–19
Introduction; Features; Food and Drink;
Short Break including the 10 Essentials

Planning pages 20–33
Before You Go; Getting There; Getting
Around; Being There

Best places to see pages 34–55
The unmissable highlights of any visit
to Normandy

Best things to do pages 56–75
Good places to have lunch; top
activities; best beaches; places to take
the children; golf courses and more

Exploring pages 76–185
The best places to visit in Normandy,
organized by area

Maps
All map references are to the maps on
the covers. For example, Dieppe has the
reference ➕ 10B – indicating the grid
square in which it is to be found

Admission prices
Inexpensive (under €5)
Moderate (€5–€10)
Expensive (over €10)

Hotel prices
Price are per room per night:
€ budget (under €50); €€ moderate
(€50–€100); €€€ expensive to luxury
(over €100)

Restaurant prices
Price for a three-course meal per person
without drinks:
€ budget (under €20); €€ moderate
(€20–€40); €€€ expensive (over €40)

Contents

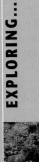

The essence of...

Normandy's greatest attraction is its variety, and each visit reveals new discoveries. The northeast coast offers old-fashioned seaside resorts, complete with mini-golf and fish stalls; the central Côte Fleurie is where up-market sun-worshippers display their jewellery; and in the west visitors can enjoy deserted dunes and wild rocky shores. Inland there are opportunities for hikers, canoeists and horse riders; and for lovers of architecture and history there's no shortage of medieval abbeys, beautiful churches, ruined castles and formidable châteaux. The only problem is deciding where the essence of Normandy lies for you.

de Pain Campagnard

e consommation

de décoration

IN DE

DIEPPE

specialist of french bread

d consomation and decoration

features

GEOGRAPHY

- 14,500km (9,010 miles) of rivers and streams.
- Longest river: the Seine.
- 600km (370 miles) of coastline.
- Highest hills: Mont des Avaloirs and the Signal d'Écouves (both 417m/1,368ft).
- Regional parks: Parc Naturel Régional de Brotonne (58,000ha/143,320 acres); Parc Naturel Régional Normandie-Maine (234,000ha/578,200 acres); Parc Naturel Régional des Marais du Cotentin et du Bessin (125,000ha/308,875 acres); Parc du Perche (182,000ha/449,720 acres).
- Regions: Haute-Normandie (upper Normandy) and Basse-Normandie (lower Normandy).
- Area: Haute-Normandie – 12,318sq km (4,755sq miles); Basse-Normandie – 17,589sq km (6,790sq miles).

POLITICS AND SOCIETY

- Five *départements* (administrative areas): Seine-Maritime and Eure (Haute-

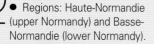

Normandie); Manche, Orne and Calvados (Basse-Normandie).

- Population: Haute-Normandie – 1,780,000; Basse-Normandie – 1,422,000; Rouen – 400,000.
- Main religion: Roman Catholicism.

TRANSPORT AND INDUSTRY

- Main economic activities: farming, fishing, tourism, textiles, oil refining.
- Major ferry ports: Cherbourg, Dieppe, le Havre and Ouistreham.
- Main bridges across the Seine: Pont de Normandie (1995) – 2,141m (7,024ft) long; Pont de Tancarville (1959) – 1,400m (4,590ft) long; Pont de Brotonne (1977) – 1,280m long (4,200ft).

SAY THE WORD

Norman place-names and family names are a mixture of Scandinavian, English and Frankish influences. The language once used by Normans has survived – just – as a patois spoken by a diminishing number on the Channel Islands. Linguists describe it as having a harder, more guttural sound than standard French, and it uses expressions derived from English and the Scandinavian languages.

food & drink

Weight-watchers are in for a tough time in Normandy. Rich dairy ingredients, mountains of fresh seafood, beef and pork and local cider are just some of the temptations in store.

DAIRY PRODUCTS

Normandy boasts some of the country's most delicious and best-known cheeses. Pont-l'Évêque, a soft and creamy cheese, is made with fresh warm milk and sold in squares. The stronger and smellier Livarot, made from staler milk, is round and banded with 'stripes' that earn it the nickname 'le colonel'. Neufchâtel is a cream cheese packaged in a variety of shapes and edible after 12 days (but better after several months). Heading the bill, though, is Camembert, now made in thousands of different versions in many corners of Europe. Normandy Camembert is the genuine article: the very best bears the

letters VCN (*véritable Camembertde Normandie*). Because of the wealth of dairy farms, Normans have a passion for cream and butter, particularly in the rural Pays d'Auge where almost any dish – fish, meat, potatoes or vegetables – can be served with a dairy sauce *à la vallée d'Auge*.

SEAFOOD

Some of the freshest and tastiest seafood you will ever sample is served up in the harbourside restaurants of the coastal resorts. The list is mouthwatering: lobsters, mussels, oysters, crabs, and a multitude of fish. *Marmite dieppoise* combines the best of all worlds: a spicy stew with shrimp, mussels and white fish; for an even more impressive concoction order an *assiette de fruits de mer*, a mixture of mussels, oysters, clams, cockles, crabs and more. The pick of the seafood eateries can be found along the quays of Dieppe, Honfleur and Granville.

MEAT AND OFFAL

Squeamish carnivores would do well to avoid asking too many questions about the local menus – especially in Rouen, where the main ingredient of *canard* (duck) *rouennais* is put through all sorts of agonies for the gourmet's benefit. In order to keep the full flavour of its blood, the unfortunate bird is either strangled or smothered; alternatively it is squeezed through a press so that the juice of its bones gives an added edge to the sauce.

Vegetarianism is a lonely calling in a region where menus include Mortagne-au-Perche's famous *boudin noir* (black pudding), Vire's *andouilles* (chitterlings), and *tripes à la mode de Caen*, which is served after stewing for several hours.

DESSERTS AND DRINKS

Apples and pears feature prominently in Norman puddings, as well as in the most celebrated drinks,

cider and calvados. Calvados, named after the *département*, is a brandy made from fermented and distilled apples matured in oak for up to 10 years. The *trou* (hole) *normand* is the custom of knocking back a small glass of calvados in the middle of a meal to stimulate the digestion. (Nowadays it's more likely to be a calvados and apple sorbet.) Perry, or *poiré*, is made from pears in the same way cider is produced from apples. Popular desserts are *douillon* (pear baked in pastry) and *bouillon* (a kind of apple dumpling).

short break

If you only have a short time to visit Normandy, or would like to get a really complete picture of the region, here are the essentials:

- **Climb to the top** of Mont-St-Michel (➤ 50–51) – it's a long haul, but well worth it for the outstanding views of the bay and the mount itself, casting its distinctive shadow across the sands.

- **Buy a snack** at a *pâtisserie:* there's one in nearly every town and village, and whatever you choose will be fresh and delicious.

- **Stroll through the beech woods** – the Forêt de Lyons, for example (➤ 109) – and enjoy their grace and silvery light.

- **Order a dish of fresh seafood** *(assiette de fruits de mer)* at a harbourside restaurant in Dieppe (➤ 118–119) or Honfleur (➤ 158).

● **Get off the beaten track** and explore the inland countryside: abbeys, châteaux and other sites are well signposted, and timber-framed farm buildings and turreted mansions can be found even along the most remote and unpromising country lanes.

● **Browse among the stalls** of one of the weekly markets, where you can find a rich assortment of fresh fruit and vegetables, live chickens and rabbits, home-baked cakes, antiques…

● **Drive to the tip of the Cotentin peninsula (Cap de la Hague)** and look out past the lighthouse for dramatic views across the English Channel (➤ 169).

- **See the 'land of horses'** from horseback (➤ 60) – or watch the best of the breeds on parade at le Haras du Pin national stud (➤ 145).

- **Cross the Seine** by ferry at Duclair, west of Rouen, or across the bow-backed Pont de Normandie, for a sense of the meandering course of the river.

- **Get a real taste of Normandy** by trying cider with your meal, a selection of the region's cheeses (➤ 12–13), and a *trou normand* – a glass of calvados between courses.

Planning

Before you go

WHEN TO GO

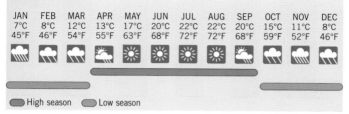

JAN	FEB	MAR	APR	MAY	JUN	JUL	AUG	SEP	OCT	NOV	DEC
7°C	8°C	12°C	13°C	17°C	20°C	22°C	22°C	20°C	15°C	11°C	8°C
45°F	46°F	54°F	55°F	63°F	68°F	72°F	72°F	68°F	59°F	52°F	46°F

High season ⬤ Low season

Normandy has a maritime climate tempered by sea breezes, which means you can expect rain any time of year, but it's most prevalent in autumn and winter. The weather is usually unpredictable, and can change very quickly.

On the whole, though, the summers are dry and warm, with generally cooler temperatures in the north of the region.

Winters tend to be mild and wet, but can be bitterly cold in December, January and February, when many hotels and places of interest are shut, especially in seaside and spa locations.

Spring is a particularly good time to travel, when the blossom is out and the weather is likely to be sunny, but not too hot.

WHAT YOU NEED

● Required
○ Suggested
▲ Not required

Some countries require a passport to remain valid for a minimum period (usually at least six months) beyond the date of entry – contact their consulate or embassy or your travel agency for details.

	UK	Germany	USA	Netherlands	Spain
Passport	●	●	●	●	●
Visa (regulations can change—check before booking your journey)	▲	▲	▲	▲	▲
Onward or Return Ticket	▲	▲	▲	▲	▲
Health Inoculations	▲	▲	▲	▲	▲
Health Documentation (➤ 23, Health Insurance)	●	●	●	●	●
Travel Insurance	○	○	○	○	○
Driving Licence (national)	●	●	●	●	●
Car Insurance Certificate (if own car)	●	●	●	●	●

WEBSITES

www.normandy-tourism.org
www.cdt-eure.fr
www.manchetourisme.com
www.calvados-tourisme.com
www.ornetourisme.com

www.seine-maritime-tourisme.com
www.rouentourisme.com
www.ville-caen.fr
www.bayeux-tourism.com
www.ville-cherbourg.fr

TOURIST OFFICES AT HOME

In the UK

French Tourist Office
178 Piccadilly, London W1V 0AL
☎ 020 7399 3500 (recorded information)

Normandy Tourist Board
The Old Bakery
Bath Hill, Keynsham

Bristol BS18 1HG
☎ 0117 986 0386

In the USA

French Government Tourist Office
444 Madison Avenue
16th floor
New York NY 10020
☎ 212/838-7800

HEALTH INSURANCE

Nationals of EU and certain other countries can get medical treatment in France at reduced cost on production of the relevant document (EHIC – European Health Insurance Card), although private medical insurance is still advised and is essential for all other visitors.

As for general medical treatment, nationals of EU countries can obtain dental treatment at reduced cost. Private medical insurance is still advisable for all.

TIME DIFFERENCES

| GMT | France | Germany | USA (NY) | Netherlands | Spain |
| 12 noon | 1PM | 1PM | 7AM | 1PM | 1PM |

France is one hour ahead of Greenwich Mean Time (GMT+1), but from late March, when clocks are put forward one hour, until late October French summer time (GMT+2) operates.

NATIONAL HOLIDAYS

1 Jan *New Year's Day*
Mar/Apr *Easter Sunday and Monday*
1 May *Labour Day*
8 May *VE Day*

May *Ascension Day*
May/Jun *Whit Sunday and Monday*
14 Jul *Bastille Day*
15 Aug *Assumption Day*

1 Nov *All Saints' Day*
11 Nov *Remembrance Day*
25 Dec *Christmas Day*

WHAT'S ON WHEN

January–April
Apple markets, Parc Naturel Régional de Brotonne (ask at tourist offices for venues).

March
Tree Fair, Lisieux (first week).
Fair celebrating Mortagne-au-Perche's traditional blood-sausage (first week).
Scandinavian Film Festival, Rouen.

April
Rouen International Fair (first two weeks).

April–May
Street Theatre Festival, Fécamp.

May
Jazz under the Apple Trees, Coutances.
Geranium Fair, Beuvron-en-Auge.
Spring Fair (religious and folk events), le Mont-St-Michel.
Jeanne d'Arc Festival, Rouen.

May–June
Seafarers' Pilgrimage, Honfleur.

June
Music Festival, venues throughout Orne.
Anniversary of Normandy Landings, D-Day Beaches (6 June).
Folklore Festival, Trouville.

June–October
Eure Summer Festival, venues throughout Eure.
July
Medieval Festival, Bayeux.
Pilgrimage across the beaches, le Mont-St-Michel.
Puppet Festival, Dives-sur-Mer.
July–August
Coutances Summer Festival.
Cheese Fair, Livarot.
August
Thoroughbred Yearling Auction and Polo Lancel Cup, Deauville.
Turkey Market, Lisieux.
Early Music Festival, Dieppe.
Les Traversées de Tatihou (traditional music and dancing), Île de Tatihou.
August–September
Presentation of stallions and horse teams of the national stud, St-Lô.
Music Festival, Orne.
Donkey racing, Trouville.
September
Sea Festival (La Mer en Fête), Le Havre.
Horse racing, parade and presentation of studs, le Haras du Pin.
Caen International Fair.
American Film Festival, Deauville.
Ancient Ste-Croix Fair, Lessay.
International Mushroom Fair, Bellême.
October
Horse Week, locations throughout Calvados.
Cider Market and Festival, Beuvron-en-Auge.
Shrimp Festival, Honfleur.
International Flower Show, Lisieux.
November
Jacques Vabre Transatlantic Race, le Havre.
Horse jumping (Jump'Orne), Alençon.
Apple Festival, le Havre.
December
Turkey Fair, Sées.

Getting there

BY AIR
Rouen Airport

7km (4 miles) to city centre

🚌	N/A
🚐	N/A
🚗	10 minutes

There are airports at Rouen, Caen, Deauville, le Havre and Cherbourg, but relatively few international flights are handled in Normandy and the most straightforward option for the majority of travellers is to fly to Paris and take an internal flight or drive from there.

Lyon, Marseille, Nice and Nantes also operate domestic flights to Normandy.

BY CAR
Driving to Normandy from neighbouring countries on mainland Europe is a relatively straightforward matter of following France's comprehensive system of *autoroutes* (motorways). Driving from the UK involves taking either the roll-on, roll-off ferry or the Eurotunnel shuttle train (➤ below).

BY TRAIN AND COACH
Drivers can take their vehicles on the Eurotunnel shuttle train, which departs from near Folkestone in Kent (M20, junction 11A), and reaches Sangatte, near Calais, in 35 minutes. Fares are charged per car and passengers stay with their vehicles during the journey. The high-speed Eurostar service

from London to Paris carries foot passengers through the Channel Tunnel, taking as little as 2 hours 35 minutes to cover the whole route. Travellers can change at Lille for services to Normandy.

Coach (long-distance bus) is an inexpensive travel option, setting off from Victoria Coach Station in London to the ferry port at Dover, and running direct to Rouen (8 hours) or Caen (10 hours).

BY FERRY

Numerous cross-Channel ferries, hovercraft and catamarans connect England's southern coast with several French ports. Norman ferry ports are Dieppe, Cherbourg, Ouistreham and le Havre. In the summer months, high-speed services sail to Cherbourg and Ouistreham.

Ferries also sail between the Irish coast and Cherbourg and le Havre. An alternative to the direct crossing is to take the shorter route to Dunkirk, Calais or Boulogne and drive from there to Normandy.

Getting around

PUBLIC TRANSPORT

Internal flights Domestic flights link Paris (Roissy-Charles de Gaulle and Orly) with Cherbourg, Rouen, Caen and le Havre.

Trains Main lines connect Paris with Rouen, le Havre, Dieppe, Caen, Cherbourg and Granville. Within Normandy there is a wide rail network linking all the main centres and many smaller towns. Free timetables are available from tourist offices.

Buses Most sizeable towns have a bus station *(gare routière)*. Some lines operate in conjunction with SNCF trains; other, local services link smaller towns and villages, and Bus verts du Calvados operate some of the longer rural lines. Apart from the regional transport lines (see Trains), timetables are quite difficult to find outside major centres such as Rouen and Caen, but times are often posted on the bus stops themselves.

Boats and ferries Fast ferries sail between Granville or Carteret and Jersey: see www.manche-iles-express.com for details. A family-run charter ferry operates three times a week (Mon, Wed, Fri) between Cherbourg and Alderney carrying up to 12 passengers per trip (www.bwcharters.net).

Urban transport Urban bus routes operate in larger cities. Rouen has a Métro that links both banks of the Seine and extends south into the suburbs. A booklet giving details is available free from the Rouen tourist office, 25 place de la Cathédrale (☎ 02 32 08 32 40).

TAXIS

Taxis are a costlier option than public transport. They pick up at taxi ranks *(stations de taxi)* found at railway stations and airports. Hotels and restaurants can usually give a taxi call number. Check the taxi has a meter; there is a pick-up charge plus a rate per minute.

FARES AND TICKETS

Students/youths An International Student Identity Card (ISIC) entitles holders to various discounts on public transport, museum admission and entertainment. Apply online at www.isic.org.

Senior citizens A number of tour companies offer special arrangements for senior citizens; for further information contact the French Tourist Office (➤ 23). Senior citizens are eligible for reduced or free entrance to sights (aged 60 and over), and discounts on public transport (aged 65 and over).

DRIVING

- The French drive on the right side of the road.
- Speed limits on toll motorways *(autoroutes)*: 130kph/80mph (110kph/68mph when wet); non-toll motorways and dual carriageways: 110kph/68mph (100kph/62mph when wet). In fog (visibility less than 50m/55yds): 50kph (31mph) all roads.
- Speed limits on country roads: 90kph/56mph (80kph/49mph when wet).
- Speed limits on urban roads: 50kph/31mph (limit starts at town sign).
- Seatbelts must be worn in front seats at all times and in rear seats where fitted. Children under 10 must sit in the back.
- Random breath-testing takes place. Never drive under the influence of alcohol.
- Petrol, including unleaded *(sans plomb)*, and diesel *(gasoil)* is widely available. Petrol stations are numerous along main roads but rarer in rural areas. Some on minor roads are closed on Sundays. Maps showing petrol stations are available from main tourist offices.
- A red warning triangle must be carried if your car has no hazard warning lights. Place the triangle 30m (33yds) behind the car in the event of an accident or breakdown. On the motorways ring from emergency phones (every 2km/1.2 miles) to contact the breakdown service. Off the motorways, police will advise on local breakdown services.

CAR RENTAL

All large towns have car-rental agencies at their airports and railway stations. Car rental is expensive, but airlines and tour operators offer fly-drive and French Railways (SNCF) train-car packages, often more economical than hiring locally.

Being there

TOURIST OFFICES
Comité Régional du Tourisme de Normandie
14 rue Charles Corbeau
27000 Évreux ☎ 02 32 33 79 00

Departmental Tourist Offices
Calvados
8 rue Renoir, 14054 Caen
☎ 02 31 27 90 30

Eure
3 rue Commandant Letellier
BP 367, 27003 Évreux
☎ 02 32 62 04 27

Eure-et-Loir
10 rue du Dr Maunoury

BP 67, 28002 Chartres cedex
☎ 02 37 84 01 01

La Manche
Route de Villedieu, 50008 St-Lô
☎ 02 33 05 98 70

Orne
86 rue St-Blaise
BP 50, 61002 Alençon
☎ 02 33 28 88 71

Seine-Maritime
6 rue Couronné
BP 60, 76420 Bihorel-les-Rouen
☎ 02 35 12 10 10

MONEY
The euro (€) is the official currency. Banknotes are in denominations of 5, 10, 20, 50, 100, 200 and 500 euros and coins are in denominations of 1, 2, 5, 10, 20 and 50 cents, and 1 and 2 euros. Euro travellers' cheques are widely accepted, as are major credit cards. Credit and debit cards can also be used for withdrawing euro notes from cashpoint machines.

TIPS/GRATUITIES

Yes ✓   No ✗

Restaurants (service included, tip optional)	✓ change
Cafés/bars (service included, tip optional)	✓ change
Taxis	✓ 10%
Chambermaids/porters	✓ €1
Tour guides	✓ €1
Toilet attendants	✓ change

POSTAL SERVICES

The PTT *(Postes et Télécommunications)* deals with mail and telephone services. Outside main centres, post offices open shorter hours and may close 12–2. Letter boxes are yellow. Open: 8am–7pm (till 12 Sat). Closed: Sun. Main post office in Rouen: 45 rue Jeanne d'Arc (☎ 02 32 76 66 20).

TELEPHONES

Telephone numbers in France comprise 10 digits; the first two for Normandy numbers are 02 (omit 0 if dialling from the UK). Many public phones use pre-paid cards *(télécartes)*; these can be bought at post offices, *bureaux de tabac* and branches of France Télécom. They come in units of 50 or 120.

International dialling codes	Emergency telephone numbers
From France:	Police: 17
UK: 00 44	Fire: 18
Germany: 00 49	Ambulance: 15
USA & Canada: 00 1	SOS Travellers: 04 91 62 12 80
Netherlands: 00 31	
Spain: 00 34	

EMBASSIES AND CONSULATES

UK ☎ 01 44 51 31 00 (Paris)
Germany ☎ 01 53 83 45 00 (Paris)
USA ☎ 01 43 12 22 22 (Paris)

Netherlands ☎ 01 40 62 33 00 (Paris)
Spain ☎ 01 44 43 18 00 (Paris)

HEALTH ADVICE

Sun advice The sunniest and hottest months are July and August, but the good weather can start in June and continue to October. Although the weather is mild, take care on the beach and when walking. Drink plenty of fluids, wear a hat and use sunscreen.

Drugs Pharmacies – recognized by their green cross sign – have qualified staff able to offer medical advice, provide first aid, and prescribe and provide a wide range of drugs, though some are available by prescription *(ordonnance)* only.

Safe water It is safe to drink tap water served in hotels and restaurants, but never drink from a tap marked *eau non potable* (not drinking water). Bottled water is cheap and widely available.

PERSONAL SAFETY

The *Police Municipale* (blue uniforms) carry out police duties in cities and towns. The *Gendarmes* (blue trousers, black jackets, white belts), the national police force, cover the countryside and smaller places. The *CRS* deal with emergencies and also look after safety on beaches.

To avoid danger or theft:

Do not use unmanned roadside rest areas at night.

Cars, especially foreign cars, should be secured.

In crowded places, beware of pickpockets.

Police assistance: ☎ 17 from any call box

ELECTRICITY

The French power supply is: 220 volts. Type of socket: round two-hole sockets taking two-round-pin (or occasionally three-round-pin) plugs. British visitors should bring an adaptor; US visitors a voltage transformer.

OPENING HOURS

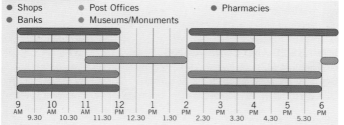

- Shops
- Banks
- Post Offices
- Museums/Monuments
- Pharmacies

In addition to the times shown above, afternoon times of shops in summer can extend in the most popular centres. Most shops close Sunday and many on Monday. Small food shops open from 7am and may open Sunday morning.

Large department stores do not close for lunch and hypermarkets open 10am to 9 or 10pm, but may shut Monday morning.

Banks are closed Sunday as well as Saturday or Monday.

Many post offices are open until 8pm.

Museums and monuments have extended summer hours. Many close one day a week: either Monday (municipal ones) or Tuesday (national ones).

LANGUAGE

French is the native language. English is spoken widely, especially in tourist areas and the larger and most popular centres; in smaller, rural places fewer people speak English. Attempts to speak French, or at least greet others in French, will be appreciated. Below is a list of helpful words. More coverage can be found in the *AA's Essential French Phrase Book*.

hotel	*l'hôtel*	reservation	*la réservation*
guest house	*chambre d'hôte*	rate	*tarif*
room	*la chambre*	breakfast	*le petit déjeuner*
single room	*une personne*	toilet	*les toilettes*
double room	*deux personnes*	bathroom	*la salle de bain*
per person	*par personne*	shower	*la douche*
per room	*par chambre*	key	*la clef/clé*
one/two nights	*une/deux nuits*	chambermaid	*femme de chambre*
bank	*la banque*	banknote	*le billet*
exchange office	*le bureau de change*	coin	*la pièce*
post office	*la poste*	credit card	*la carte de crédit*
cashier	*le caissier*	travellers' cheque	*le chèque de voyage*
foreign exchange	*le change extérieur*	exchange rate	*le taux de change*
English pound	*la livre sterling*		
restaurant/café	*la restaurant/le café*	starter	*l'hors d'œuvre*
table	*la table*	main course	*le plat principal*
menu	*le menu*	dish of the day	*le plat du jour*
set menu	*le menu du jour*	dessert	*le dessert*
wine list	*la carte des vins*	drink	*la boisson*
lunch/dinner	*le déjeuner/le dîner*	the bill	*'addition*
yes/no	*oui/non*	yesterday	*hier*
please/thank you	*s'il vous plaît/merci*	how much?	*combien?*
hello/goodbye	*bonjour/au revoir*	expensive	*cher*
goodnight	*bonsoir*	open/closed	*ouvert/fermé*
sorry/excuse me	*pardon/excusez-moi*	you're welcome	*de rien*
help!	*au secours!*	okay	*d'accord*
today/tomorrow	*aujourd'hui/demain*	I don't know	*je ne sais pas*

Best places to see

1 Abbaye de Jumièges

www.jumieges.fr

Once a centre of scholarship and worship, this magnificent abbey was plundered after the French Revolution and is now a haunting ruin.

With its soaring white towers, circled by rooks, Jumièges has a strangely unsettling effect. The earliest ruins – the Église St-Pierre – date from the 10th century when the Benedictine abbey was refounded to replace the 7th-century original

burned by Vikings. In 1040 work began on a second church, Notre-Dame, consecrated in the presence of Duke William the Bastard. During the following 300 years Jumièges prospered, accumulating gifts and adding new buildings.

With the Hundred Years War Jumièges entered a period of insecurity and slow decline; by 1792 there were only seven resident monks and the abbey was closed. It then passed to a series of private owners: one tried to set up a factory in it; another blew up the chancel and sold off the stone. Only in 1824 did new owners put a halt to the destruction.

Notre-Dame is the most spectacular part of the former monastic complex. Its twin western towers – once with timber spires – flank the entrance into a vast roofless nave lined with bold arcades. Beyond the transepts, where the northwest column has an intricate carving of a bird, a delicate 13th-century lancet arch marks the site of the chancel chapels. 'Charles VII's Passageway' leads to the Église St-Pierre, whose own towers have now gone except for their rectangular bases. Only the outline remains of the cloisters. Behind the abbey, a flight of curving steps leads up to the 17th-century abbot's lodgings, still intact, and a small knot-garden.

✚ 9D ✉ 27km (17 miles) ☎ 02 35 37 24 02 🕐 Mid-Apr to mid-Sep daily 9:30–7; mid-Sep to mid-Apr daily 9:30–1, 2:30–5:30 ✋ Inexpensive (free 1st Sun in month Oct–Apr) 🍴 Auberge des Ruines (€€), place de la Mairie 🚌 30 from Rouen (change buses at Duclair)

2 Les Andelys & Château Gaillard

www.ville-andelys.fr

A historic timber-framed village lies at the foot of the hill where Richard the Lionheart's castle has panoramic views over the Seine Valley.

Situated on the edge of a deep loop in the Seine, at the northern end of the Forêt des Andelys, are the two towns of les Andelys. Petit Andely grew in the shadow of King Richard's castle while Grand Andely is a busy centre with a Saturday market. The ruins of **Château Gaillard** rise from a high chalk outcrop; from a distance they are barely distinguishable from

the white cliffs. Richard had the castle hastily constructed – probably between 1196 and 1198 – though it became known as his 'one-year wonder' because of the speed with which it was built.

One of the five original towers still stands, as well as part of the donjon, the later governor's lodge and the curtain walls. While these squat remains still preserve an impenetrable appearance, the château fell to the French just six years after its completion, when King Philippe Auguste's soldiers entered through the latrines.

Below Château Gaillard, Petit Andely extends along the riverside, a fine collection of stone and timber buildings with carved lintels, coloured glass and swirling iron lampholders. Galleries and restaurants line the street, leading into a peaceful cobbled square overlooked by the Église St-Sauveur. Grand Andely itself has some fine town houses, as well as the 13th- to 17th-century Église Notre-Dame. The Musée Nicolas Poussin houses paintings by the artist, and the Mémorial Normandie-Niémen commemorates General de Gaulle's fighter squadron.

➕ 11E 🍴 Choice of restaurants (€–€€€) 🚌 From Évreux, marked 'les Andelys'

Château Gaillard

☎ 02 32 54 04 16 🕒 Mid-Mar to mid-Nov Wed–Mon 10–1, 2–6 💷 Inexpensive

3 Bayeux Tapestry

www.bayeux-tourism.com

All the colour, character and action of a good film are captured in this 70m-long (76yd) tapestry, commissioned to celebrate William the Conqueror's victory at Hastings.

William's half-brother Odo, Bishop of Bayeux, decided to decorate his new cathedral with a spectacular wall-hanging to impress pilgrims and local people coming to the church. A team of embroiderers took several years to complete the frieze in eight different-coloured wools. The result, now displayed in a former seminary, traces the Norman dispute over the English royal inheritance. It begins with the aged King Edward sending his brother-in-law Earl Harold Godwinson to Normandy to inform William (allegedly) that he will be the next English king. Harold's adventures include shipwreck, capture and rescue, and a thrilling ride with William's troops against the Duke of Brittany.

Before seeing the tapestry, visitors are led past a long but useful exhibition, which suggests that the tapestry deliberately includes flashbacks and split-screen effects for dramatic impact. An audio-visual commentary then guides you all too quickly past the genuine article. The wealth of detail deserves a much longer browse: spies listening to royal conversations; the Saxons sporting droopy moustaches; Halley's Comet shooting ominously over Harold's coronation; food and wine being loaded for the invasion fleet; and, in the final battle scenes, horses mustering, galloping and falling while, in the tapestry margins, soldiers' corpses are stripped of their armour. It's so fresh and energetic that you can almost hear the din of a battle fought over 900 years ago.

✠ 5D ✉ Centre Guillaume le Conquérant, rue de Nesmond, Bayeux ☎ 02 31 51 25 50 🕐 Mid-Mar to Apr, Sep–Oct daily 9–6:30; Nov to mid-Mar daily 9:30–12:30, 2–6; May–Aug 9–7. Closed 1 Jan, 25 Dec and 2 weeks in Jan 🖐 Moderate 🍴 Choice of restaurants in town (€–€€)

4 Château d'O

Mirrored in the waters of its moat, the towers and pointed roofs of Château d'O give it a fairy-tale charm.

This romantic château was built in 1484 for Jean d'O, Charles VIII's chamberlain, on the foundations of an 11th-century fortress. In 1590 a western wing was added by Jean's powerful descendant, François d'O. Having risen from governor of Caen to Henri

III's superintendent of finance, François manoeuvred his way through the controversy and changing alliances of the Religious Wars, and emerged as Henri IV's counsellor. During his career he was accused of pocketing royal funds for his own use – partly to spend on this family seat.

Elaborate carvings decorate the oldest part of the château, the gatehouse, while an arcade and windows with decorative iron grilles line the 16th-century south wing. Red and black brick patterns occasionally break the pale gold and grey stone of the façade, and the O family emblem, the ermine, is carved on the south wing. A walkway leads across the moat into a three-sided courtyard, with further intricate carvings decorating the walls. Inside, the furnishings date mainly from the 18th century, and include *trompe l'œils* of Apollo and the Nine Muses as eagles in flight, uncovered in the west wing during renovation work. The château grounds are as tranquil as the building itself: a path leads through the simple garden to woodland, and past the chapel to the orangery where exhibitions are occasionally held. Beyond the south wing, the farm buildings that once housed some of the château's household are now a restaurant.

🕇 19J ☎ 02 33 35 34 69 ❸ Open selected afternoons during the summer. Telephone for details 👋 Free 🍽 La Ferme du Château d'O (€€–€€€) ☎ 02 33 35 36 87 🚌 From Alençon to Mortrée

5 Dieppe

www.dieppetourisme.com

This energetic, modern harbour town, with its delightful old quarters, offers visitors arriving by ferry a compelling first taste of France.

There's something irresistibly cheerful about Dieppe, even though it could do with a coat of paint. Once cross-Channel ferries deposited passengers opposite the quai Henri IV's hotels and restaurants, where they could then tuck into fresh seafood while watching the latest catch being unloaded on to quayside stalls. Now the ferry terminal has been shifted out of sight, yachts have moved in, and the fish stalls have been moved aside to make way for a car park. But there is still a lively pulse to the town, especially in the pedestrianized centre.

Across the water from the end of quai Henri IV the clifftop Église Notre-Dame de Bon-Secours watches over the port. The road swings round to the shingle beach where grand old houses line boulevard de Verdun and, in summer, stalls are set out along boulevard du Maréchal Foch, which runs parallel. Looming over all at the west end of the town is the 15th-century castle, whose **Musée du Château** houses a collection of carved ivory – a speciality of Dieppe in the 17th century – and paintings by Renoir, Boudin, Pissarro and Braque.

Narrow alleys lined with crumbling old houses lead from the promenade and quayside into the centre of town and to the 14th- to 16th-century

Église St-Jacques, its fabric slowly being eaten away by the elements. Inside is a frieze of Brazilian natives rescued from the palace of Jean Ango, François I's naval adviser, whose fleet of privateers captured more than 300 Portuguese ships in the 16th century. Northeast, in the old fishing quarter, the **Cité de la Mer** has exhibitions on shipbuilding, sea life and geology.

✚ 10B 🍴 Choice of seafood restaurants on quai Henri IV (€–€€) 🚌 From Rouen

Musée du Château

✉ Rue Chastes ☎ 02 35 06 61 99 🕐 Jun–Sep daily 10–12, 2–6; Oct–May Wed–Mon 10–12, 2–5 (Sun 6). Closed 1 Jan, 1 May, 1 Nov, 25 Dec ✋ Inexpensive

Cité de la Mer

✉ Rue del'Asile Thomas ☎ 02 3506 93 20 🕐 Daily 10–12, 2–6. Closed 25 Dec–1 Jan ✋ Inexpensive

Honfleur

This is one of the prettiest and most popular harbour towns in Normandy, with an old-world ambience and a distinguished maritime history.

Honfleur is about as attractive as a working port can be. Tall grey houses stand shoulder-to-shoulder along the Vieux Bassin (Old Dock), the focus of the town, fishing boats cluster along the harbour near by, and shops, galleries, restaurants and hotels fill the many timber-framed and slate-fronted buildings.

The port has a long history. Its heyday as a seafaring centre was in the 17th century, when Samuel de Champlain set sail to found Québec; his achievement is noted on a plaque on the wall of the 16th-century Lieutenance, a ramshackle stone

building guarding the harbour entrance, and once the home of the king's lieutenant, the governor of Honfleur. Église Ste-Catherine in the market place is remarkable for its construction by shipbuilders using wooden struts and tiles for both the main body and the 18m (59ft) bell tower that stands alone across the square. The 15th-century church is dark but airy, like a great barn: two parallel naves are divided by slender

timber columns and the vaulted ceiling has the look of an upturned boat. The second nave was added in 1496 to accommodate the prosperous town's growing population of sailors and ship-owners.

Not surprisingly, Honfleur was a magnet to artists in the 19th and 20th centuries. The **Musée Eugène Boudin,** named after the town's most famous son, has works by Dufy, Corot, Monet and the man himself.

🚌 8D 🍴 Choice of restaurants and cafés (€–€€€) 🚌 From Caen and le Havre

Musée Eugène Boudin
✉ Rue de l'Homme-de-Bois, place Erik-Satie ☎ 02 31 89 54 00 🕐 Mid-Mar to Sep Wed–Mon 10–12, 2–6; Oct to mid-Mar Wed–Mon 2:30–5, weekend 10–12, 2:30–5. Closed 1 Jan–10 Feb ✋ Moderate

7 Le Mémorial, Caen

www.memorial-caen.fr

Outstanding among Normandy's many war museums, this 'Museum for Peace' examines the events leading up to World War II and looks into an uncertain future.

Across the limestone façade of le Mémorial runs the inscription: *'La douleur m'a brisée, la fraternité m'a relevée…de ma blessure a jailli un fleuve de liberté'* ('Grief crushed me, fraternity revived me…from my wound there sprang a river of freedom'). Conflict and hope are the themes of this museum. Hovering over the vast entrance hall is a British Hawker Typhoon aircraft; a caption notes that its 23-year-old pilot was killed when it was shot down in 1944. This is not a museum of military hardware or cold strategy: throughout its themed 'spaces' individual experience is set against the progress of world affairs. Spaces One to Three trace events from 1918 to 1944 along a spiralling walkway that descends into near-darkness. Archive material includes letters, film, photographs and a secretly taped phone conversation between the collaborator Weygand and his delegate to the armistice talks. There are harrowing images: the hopeless faces of

concentration camp victims; a 17-year-old Russian patriot about to be hanged.

Beyond the walkway, displays include personal letters and footage of hand-to-hand fighting during the German advance on Stalingrad. In spaces Four and Five documentary and fictional film recreates the 1944 invasion. Post-war conflict and diplomacy are covered in Jacques Perrin's film *Hope* in Space Six, and the final space is a gallery devoted to winners of the Nobel Peace Prize.

✚ 6E ✉ Esplanade du Général Eisenhower ☎ 02 31 06 06 44 🕐 Jul–Aug 9–8; Sep, Oct, mid-Feb to Jun 9–6; Nov to mid-Feb 9–7. Closed 25 Dec, 2 weeks in Jan. Last entry 75 mins before closing 💷 Expensive 🍽 Restaurant and café (€€) 🚌 From Tour le Roy in Caen centre

8 Le Mont-St-Michel

www.ot-montsaintmichel.com

Across its broad bay, le Mont-St-Michel rises like a mirage, tapering up to the abbey spire from a chaotic pyramid of houses and shops.

In the early 8th century Bishop Aubert of Avranches had a vision in which the Archangel Michael ordered him to build a sanctuary on the isolated granite rock then known as Mont Tombé. This was no mean feat: apart from the problem of building on a sheer, narrow rock, the island is isolated by quicksands at low tide and deep water at high tide. Nevertheless,

Aubert's church was finished in AD708, and in the 10th century a monastery was founded on the site. Over the centuries new buildings were added to the abbey and a town grew beneath it, clinging precariously to the steep sides. Buttresses and massive walls clamp everything fast to the rock, the church towering above the sands that have claimed the lives of many pilgrims on the last leg of their journey. Now the Mont is approached across a causeway and through the Porte du Roi. The winding Grande Rue, lined with souvenir shops and cafés, climbs towards the abbey, and steps lead off through narrow passages to the outer ramparts. Finally, all routes lead to the **Abbaye** itself and the buildings known as 'la Merveille'. A trail passes through the refectory, cloisters and Knights' Hall, and past a huge wooden treadmill once operated by inmates when the abbey became a prison in the 18th century; the wheel was used to haul supplies straight up a steep ramp. Eventually steps lead down into the crypt where 10 massive columns support the abbey church. Outside, a tiny herb garden squeezed among turrets and chimneys looks out across the bay. There are several museums on the Mont, as well as the Logis Tiphaine, home of the 14th-century military commander Bertrand du Guesclin.

✚ 14J 🍴 La Mère Poulard (€€), Grand Rue 🚌 From Granville and Pontorson

Abbaye

☎ 02 33 89 80 00 🕔 May–Aug daily 9–7 (last admission 6); Sep–Apr 9:30–6 (last admission 5). Closed 1 Jan, 1 May, 25 Dec 🖐 Moderate

Musée des Beaux-Arts André Malraux, le Havre

www.lehavretourisme.com

This striking modern building, with its highly original walls of glass, houses an excellent display of French paintings.

Le Havre can be an oppressive place, with its endless apartment blocks and the concrete centre erected quickly after the devastation of the old town by air raids in 1944 (➤ 108). For anyone interested in Normandy's artistic heritage, though, it has the best gallery in the region. Named after the novelist and art critic André Malraux (1901–76), the museum makes the most of its view over the port (through a large concrete sculpture nicknamed 'The Eye') and uses light and space to the best advantage in its open galleries.

Malraux devised the concept of 'the museum without walls', and this building comes as near as

possible to fulfilling that idea. One feature is that visitors can choose how to view the paintings: chronologically from the 17th to the 20th centuries, or beginning with the famous collection of works by Eugène Boudin (1824–98) and Raoul Dufy (1877–1953).

Boudin, who was born near by in Honfleur, represents French Impressionism along with Monet, Renoir and others. His love of painting out in the open, using free brushwork to convey the coast's huge skies and seas, earned him the title 'painter of beaches' and provided inspiration for Monet. Dufy was a native of le Havre and one of the group of fauvist ('wild beast') painters who used bold colours to depict everyday scenes. Other artists featured include Corot, Manet, Millet and Courbet, and 17th- to 19th-century Dutch, Flemish and Italian painters.

✚ *Le Havre 2c* ✉ 2 boulevard Clémenceau ☎ 02 35 19 62 62 🕙 Mon, Wed, Thu, Fri 11–6; Sat, Sun 11–7 ✋ Inexpensive 🍴 Café (€€)

10 Rue du Gros-Horloge, Rouen

At the heart of Rouen's old town, this street is both a lively shopping centre and a showpiece of restored historic buildings.

There is much to admire along this pedestrianized route, where timber-framed houses have been smartly repaired, their woodwork painted in reds, pale orange and greens. The Gros-Horloge itself is an elaborate one-handed clock that sits on a stone archway spanning the street. It was originally set in the Tour du Beffroi (Belfry Tower) next door, but the citizens complained that it was too difficult to see; so in 1527 the arch was purpose-built and the clock moved. Despite its single hand, the Gros-Horloge manages to tell the

time in hours, weeks and phases of the moon. The arch is covered in baroque carvings, including Christ the Shepherd and his flock. The renovated clock and tower can be seen during the day, and guided tours take place after dark.

The rue du Gros-Horloge links the two main focal points of old Rouen. At the west end is the place du Vieux-Marché where Jeanne d'Arc (Joan of Arc) was burned at the stake in 1431. The Église Ste-Jeanne d'Arc that marks the spot is one of Rouen's most evocative modern buildings: its wildly twisted cone of a roof extends to cover part of the central market in a design said to represent the flames that ended Joan's life. At the other end of the street is the cathedral square, dominated by the cathedral itself and surrounded by several fine buildings including the city's oldest surviving Renaissance house, now the tourist office.

✚ *Rouen 2c* 🍴 Choice of restaurants and cafés, especially in and around place du Vieux-Marché (€–€€€) 🚌 From Dieppe 🚊 From le Havre, Caen, Dieppe

Gros-Horloge
🕐 Jan–Mar Tue–Sun 2–5; Apr–Oct Tue–Sun 10–6 ✋ Moderate

Best things to do

Good places to have lunch

Auberge de Goury (€–€€)

At the tip of the Cotentin peninsula, opposite a lifeboat station and lighthouse. Grills, seafood; closed Sunday evening and Monday evening.

✉ Goury, Cap de la Hague ☎ 02 33 52 77 01

Auberge St-Maclou (€–€€)

Particularly good-value set menus at lunchtime in an old Rouen building near Église St-Maclou.

✉ 222 rue Martainville, Rouen ☎ 02 35 71 06 67

Camomille (€€)

This *salon de thé* serves omelettes and generous salads, along with a good range of teas and pastries.

✉ 23 rue de Grenoble, Évreux ☎ 02 32 38 30 90

La Marine (€–€€)

Fresh seafood in a traditional restaurant overlooking the fish
market and river.

✉ 146 boulevard Fernand-Moureaux, Trouville ☎ 02 31 88 12 51

Le Pavé d'Auge (€€–€€€)

Game dishes, meat with cider and pan-fried oysters in the old
timber-framed market hall.

✉ Place du Village, Beuvron-en-Auge ☎ 02 31 79 26 71

La Régence (€€)

Popular seafood restaurant (part of the Hôtel la Régence; ➤ 182),
with good views of the harbour and fishing boats.

✉ 42 quai de Caligny, Cherbourg ☎ 02 33 43 05 16

Les Roches Blanches (€–€€)

Seafood with a fine sea view in a long building tucked under
the cliff.

✉ Terrasse Boudin, front de la mer, Étretat ☎ 02 35 27 07 34

La Taverne de Maître Kanter (€€)

Brasserie serving salads, grills, sauerkrauts and seafood. Open
midday to midnight.

✉ 1 avenue du 6 Juin, Caen ☎ 02 31 50 02 22

Les Terrasses Poulard (€–€€)

Omelettes and seafood on the mount, with spectacular bay views.

✉ 18 Grande Rue, le Mont-St-Michel ☎ 02 33 60 14 09

Le Vieux Honfleur (€€–€€€)

Outdoor tables overlooking the harbour, with especially fine
seafood on the menu.

✉ 13 quai St-Étienne, Honfleur ☎ 02 31 89 15 31

Top activities

Canoeing on the Suisse Normande rivers, particularly the fast-flowing Orne.

Cycling along the Seine Valley, the Eure Valley and the Côte d'Albâtre; also in the forests of Brotonne and Lyons.

Fishing – sea fishing from resorts along the coast; also inland on lakes and rivers. Membership of angling associations and details of permits available at each *département* tourist office.

Golf – 27-hole courses open to amateurs at Deauville, Étretat and Granville; 18-hole courses at Cabourg, Caen, Clécy, Houlgate, Deauville, Dieppe, Évreux, le Havre and Rouen (two); nine-hole courses at Bagnoles and Cherbourg (➤ 72–73).

Horse racing – courses at Alençon, Argentan, Caen, Deauville, Lisieux and Rouen, among many others.

Horse riding – treks and rides organized by centres throughout the region; along the shores of Calvados and Manche, and through woodlands and countryside in Eure and Orne.

Thalassotherapy (sea-water therapy) along the Côte Fleurie, especially in Deauville, Luc-sur-Mer, Ouistreham and Trouville; also Dieppe and Granville.

Walking on footpaths along the Seine, between Étretat and le Tréport, and across the Parc Naturel Régional Normandie-Maine and the Cotentin peninsula. There are also steeper hikes in the Suisse Normande.

Windsurfing – good, long beaches on the coastline of Calvados and western Manche.

Yachting – marinas or moorings at Barfleur, Barneville-Carteret, Cabourg, Deauville, Dieppe, Granville, Fécamp, le Havre, Honfleur, Ouistreham, St-Valéry-en-Caux and le Tréport.

⓪ through the southern forests

a drive

This long circular drive passes through the Parc Naturel Régional Normandie-Maine and southern Normandy's ancient forests.

From Alençon, take the D311 east through the Forêt de Perseigne. At the roundabout before Mamers follow signs for Bellême (D311/D955).

Beyond the woods the road leads through gentle countryside into the Perche, with its extensive fields and pasture.

At the roundabout before Bellême turn left on to the D938 through the Forêt de Bellême, heading north to Mortagne-au-Perche. Beyond Mortagne's market hall turn right (D8).

The route passes through hamlets, pastureland and the Forêt de Réno-Valdieu to Longny-au-Perche. Here, a long flight of steps leads to the 16th-century Chapelle de Notre-Dame de Pitié, and the 16th-century tower of Église St-Martin overlooks the central square.

In the centre turn left (D918) to pass through the Forêt du Perche to Randonnai. Turn left at the traffic lights (D603).

The road leads between the Forêts du Perche and de la Trappe; a series of lakes can be glimpsed through the trees. A crucifix stands above the road as it reaches a fork. Take the right fork (Rond de Trappe), but be careful: deer are still hunted here.

Emerging on to the D930, turn right, then first left to the Abbaye de la Trappe.

Founded in 1140, the abbey has an audio-visual display describing the life of Trappist monks.

Turn left on a minor road to Prépotin; then left to a T-junction and right (D930). Turn right on to the N12. At the roundabout join the D8 to Sées (▶ 154). Take the D908 to a crossroads and turn left (D26) through the Forêt d'Écouves and back to Alençon.

Distance About 205km (127 miles)
Time 3–4 hours without stops
Start/end point Alençon ✚ 19K
Lunch Le Grenier à Sel (€€) ✉ 9 rue Contcacune, Mortagne-au-Perche ☎ 02 33 25 51 98

Top souvenir ideas

It's worth looking beyond the high street for many of the traditional Norman goods. Factories and farm shops are often the best places to buy cheese, cider, honey, calvados, vegetables and fruit, as well as pottery, knitwear and gifts.

Bénédictine
This liqueur, made to an original 16th-century recipe, makes an excellent souvenir and is sold at the original distillery at Fécamp.

Boudin noir
The famous black sausage produced in Mortagne-au-Perche is best bought at the town's annual *boudin* festival in March; otherwise try and catch the Saturday morning farmers' market.

Calvados
Many local producers sell this delicious apple brandy. A glass midway through a meal is said to aid digestion. Alternatives are Pommeau (apple juice with Calvados) or cider, also on sale all over the region.

Cheese
Take your pick from Camembert, Livarot, Pont-l'Évêque or any number of lesser-known goat's or cow's milk cheeses.

Children's fashions
Pretty and stylish children's clothes in bright, cheerful colours are a French speciality.

Chocolates
Enjoy the beautiful displays in the *chocolateries* before making your selection of mouthwatering treats.

Copper pots
For an unusual gift, browse the pots and pans produced in Villedieu-les-Poêles – you might even see them being made.

Faience
Blue-and-white decorated ceramics are the speciality of Rouen, and several shops in the city centre sell interesting pieces.

Knitwear
Smart and functional woollies can be found in several outlets, and the Tricoterie du Val de Saire label is Cotentin-based.

Lace
Keep an eye out for *point d'Alençon*, along with many other examples of lacework for sale.

Best beaches

Arromanches-les-Bains – wide views taking in the Mulberry Harbour and two museums relating the D-Day landings along this stretch of coast (➤ 133).

Barfleur – a beach leads from the busy fishing harbour to one of Normandy's tallest lighthouses (➤ 168).

Barneville-Carteret – traditional seafront pleasures at two side-by-side contrasting resorts (➤ 168).

Cap de la Hague – an area of windswept walks and rugged coastal views (➤ 169).

Carolles – a sandy beach with spectacular views along the coast to Granville (➤ 170).

Deauville – a touch of glamour at this stylish north coast seaside town, complete with its famous beach huts and promenade (➤ 142).

Étretat – an attractive shingle beach extending between two striking chalk cliffs – the Falaise d'Aval and the Falaise d'Amont (➤ 100–101).

Les Salines – popular beach backed by dunes, north of Granville, but few facilities and there is limited access at high tide.

Le Tréport – a cheerful seaside resort with a shingle beach (➤ 111).

Trouville – Deauville's less up-market neighbour and a great choice for families (➤ 155).

Places to take the children

SEINE-MARITIME AND EURE
Le Canyon
Fifty rides and games, including Wild West fun and water slides.
✉ Epretot, 15km (9 miles) northeast of le Havre, off N15 ☎ 02 35 20 42 69
🕐 Jun–Aug daily 10:30–7; Mar–May, Sep to mid-Nov Wed and weekends
🖐 Moderate

Parc du Bocasse
A family park with 80 games and rides, an enchanted river, pedalos
and its very own 'Niagara Falls'.
✉ Southwest of Clères, on D6 ☎ 02 35 33 22 25 🕐 Apr–Sep daily 10–6
🖐 Expensive

CALVADOS AND ORNE
Aquarium Écologique
No fewer than 60 tanks with tropical and local fish, and several
varieties of shark. Also creepy-crawlies and reptiles, including Big
Hug, a 6m (19ft) python.
✉ 17 rue de Paris, Trouville ☎ 02 31 88 46 04 🕐 Easter–Jun, Sep, Oct daily
10–12, 2–7; Jul, Aug daily 10–7:30; Nov–Easter daily 2–6:30 🖐 Moderate

Festyland
Plenty of choice for the energetic: bouncy castles, water
rides and slides, go-karts and toboggans.
✉ Bretteville-sur-Odon, outskirts of Caen ☎ 02 31 75 04 04
🕐 Jul–Aug daily 10–7; Apr–Jun, Sep hours vary
🖐 Expensive

La Maison de la Mer
A journey through the sea tunnel leads to views of
undersea life; the shell collection is worth visiting.
✉ 20km (12 miles) northwest of Caen ☎ 02 31 37 92 58
🕐 Feb–Sep daily from 9:30 or 10 (low season); Oct, Nov,
Jan daily 2–6. Closed Dec 🖐 Inexpensive

Musée du Chemin de Fer Miniature

Claimed to be one of the largest model railways in Europe. Little locomotives – 220 of them – thunder along 430m (1,400ft) of track around a scaled-down version of the Suisse Normande. A slightly larger train carries children round the grounds (➤ 141).

✉ D562, 38km (23 miles) southwest of Caen ☎ 02 31 69 07 13
🕐 Easter–Sep daily 10–12, 2–6 or 6:30; in low season Sun 2–5. Closed Dec–early Mar 🖐 Inexpensive

LA MANCHE

L'Aquarium du Roc

Fish, shells and models; same opening times and charges as the Féerie des Coquillages (shell palace and light show), and the Palais Minéral et Jardin des Papillons (minerals, butterflies).

✉ Boulevard Vaufleury, Granville ☎ 02 33 50 19 83 🕐 Daily 9–7:30
🖐 Moderate

La Cité de la Mer

Although mainly concerned with man's adventures at sea, among the attractions is Europe's tallest cylindrical aquarium. Known as the Abyss, it offers a glimpse of life beneath the waters (➤ 172).

✉ Gare Maritime Transatlantique, Cherbourg ☎ 08 25 33 50 50 🕐 Jan–Apr, Oct–Dec daily 10–6; May, Jun, Sep 9:30–6; Jul, Aug 9–7 🖐 Expensive

Reptilarium du Mont-St-Michel

As well as the appeal of crocodiles and iguanas, pythons and boas, children can explore tunnels, ladders, a suspension bridge, pyramids, towers and a maze. The reptilarium is situated at Beauvoir, on the mainland opposite the mount.

✉ Route de Pontorson, le Mont-St-Michel ☎ 02 33 68 11 18 🕐 Apr–Sep daily 10–7; Oct–Mar 2–6 weekends and public hols only 🖐 Moderate

Stunning views

- Seine Valley, from Château Gaillard (➤ 38).

- Rouvre Valley and Suisse Normande, from the rocky outcrop of the Roche d'Oëtre (➤ 152).

- Across the Bay of le Mont-St-Michel, from the top of the abbey (➤ 50).

- Vire Valley, from the Roches de Ham (➤ 180–181).

- The Baie d'Écalgrain and towards the Channel Islands, from Nez de Jobourg.

- Côte de Nacre, from the clifftop Pointe du Hoc (➤ 149).

- Côte d'Albâtre (Alabaster Coast), from the Falaise d'Amont (➤ 101).

- Orne Valley, from Pain de Sucre, near Clécy (➤ 141).

- Hilltop spires of Coutances' Gothic cathedral, on the northern approach to the town (➤ 173).

- Remains of the Benedictine Abbaye de Hambye, in the Sienne Valley (➤ 166).

Golf courses

The Golfing Passport is a scheme operated in Calvados that allows use of five green fees on five different courses (from a selection of six) on nine consecutive days. It must be booked in advance, though no payment is due until you arrive at the first golf course. Obtain the passport from Calvados Tourisme ✉ 8 rue Renoir, 14054 Caen ☎ 02 31 27 90 30

CAEN
Golf de Caen 'Le Vallon'
A 27-hole course with a putting green, practice course, restaurant and clubhouse.

✉ 14112 Biéville-Beuville, 8km (5 miles) north of Caen ☎ 02 31 94 72 09

CHERBOURG
La Glacerie
Six indoor and 12 outdoor practice greens, plus a 9-hole course. Golf practice schools Wednesday and Saturday.

✉ Domaines des Roches, la Glacerie, 4km (2.5 miles) southeast of Cherbourg, on D122 ☎ 02 33 44 45 48

CLÉCY
Golf de Clécy-Cantelou
Eighteen holes on the manor green, plus a putting green, clubhouse and restaurant.

✉ Manoir de Cantelou, 30km (18 miles) south of Caen on D562 ☎ 02 31 69 72 72

DEAUVILLE
Golf Barrière de Deauville
Open daily (except Tue in winter), this 27-hole course also has a training green, golf shop and restaurant.

✉ 2km (1.2 miles) south of Deauville, off D278 ☎ 02 31 14 24 24

DIEPPE
Golf de Dieppe
Established in 1897, this is one of Normandy's oldest golf courses; 18 holes.

✉ 51 route de Pourville, off D75 ☎ 02 35 84 25 05

Golf de Garcelles
Two 9-hole courses, with a training bunker and putting green.

✉ Route de Lorguichon, Garcelles-Secqueville, 6km (4 miles) south of Caen
☎ 02 31 39 09 09

GRANVILLE
Golf de Granville
27 holes along the seafront on a course created in 1912, plus a covered practice course and two putting greens.

✉ 3km (2 miles) north of Granville at Bréville-sur-Mer, on D236/GR223
☎ 02 33 50 23 06

LE HAVRE
Golf du Havre
An 18-hole course dating from the 1930s.

✉ Octeville-sur-Mer, 10km (6 miles) north of le Havre ☎ 02 35 46 36 50

ROUEN
Golf de Rouen
The city's 18-hole golf club, founded in 1911.

✉ Rue Francis Poulenc, Mont-St-Aignon, 5km (3 miles) north of Rouen
on D43 ☎ 02 35 74 53 46

Places to stay

L'Absinthe (€€€)

An upmarket and expensive hotel set in a former 16th-century presbytery in the old town. Comfortable characterful rooms with exposed beams. Restaurant.
✉ 1 rue de la Ville, Honfleur ☎ 02 31 89 23 23 🕐 Closed 14 Nov–31 Dec

Best Western le Dauphin (€€–€€€)

A restored 12th-century priory with rooms in the old building and a modern annexe. Traditional, country-style restaurant and separate breakfast room.
✉ 29 rue Gémare, Caen ☎ 02 31 86 22 26

Côté Jardin (€–€€)

Excellent bed-and-breakfast in an old house on the main street. Double rooms in an annexe entered through a pretty courtyard. Breakfast served inside or out. Evening meals by arrangement.
✉ 62 rue Grande, Orbec ☎ 02 31 32 77 99

France (€€)

A traditional Logis de France hotel set in a quiet location within the centre of Évreux. The pleasant rooms are augmented by a very good restaurant offering classic dishes and fine wines.
✉ 29 rue St-Thomas, Évreux ☎ 02 32 39 09 25

Grand Hôtel (€€€)

An upmarket seafront hotel in the grand old tradition, which makes the most of its connections with Proust.
✉ Promenade Marcel Proust, Cabourg ☎ 02 31 91 01 79

Hôtel de la Cathédrale (€€–€€€)

An old building with a pretty courtyard and traditional but fresh decor, near the cathedral and archbishop's palace. Not easily accessible by car, but a place of genuine character – among some

of Rouen's best medieval houses – and run with friendly, attentive charm. No restaurant, but there is a tea room.

✉ 12 rue St-Romain, Rouen
☎ 02 35 71 57 95

Hôtel la Croix Blanche (€€–€€€)

Well-known hotel on the ramparts with spectacular views of the bay, and a restaurant with good-value menus (➤ 184). Rooms, however, can be expensive.

✉ Grande Rue, le Mont-St-Michel ☎ 02 33 60 14 03 🕙 Closed mid-Nov to mid-Feb

Hôtel le Fruitier (€–€€)

Well-run Logis de France hotel and restaurant, open all year. Modern, comfortable rooms with stylish decor and welcoming staff.

✉ Place des Costils, Villedieu-les-Poëles ☎ 02 33 90 51 00

Hôtel le Grand Large (€–€€€)

Modern building set on the cliff overlooking the sea; includes a sea-therapy centre. Parking, swimming pool, jacuzzi, bar. Wide price range for rooms. Apartments also available.

✉ 5 rue de la Falaise, Granville ☎ 02 33 91 19 19

Hôtel du Lion d'Or (€€–€€€)

Long-established hotel in an old coaching inn with a courtyard, near the centre. Bright, comfortable rooms and a restaurant.

✉ 71 rue St-Jean, Bayeux ☎ 02 31 92 06 90 🕙 Closed mid-Dec to late Jan

Exploring

Normandy is a region that defies any simple description. Its long coastline takes in family resorts, lonely windswept dunes and rocky cliffs, while inland there are marshlands, deep river gorges and gentle farmland.

Time often seems to have frozen in the villages and ancient woodlands, in the crumbling abbey ruins that tell a turbulent story of religious fervour, scholarly debate and revolutionary destruction. A solid donjon, an elegant château or a market town's startlingly elaborate parish church all speak of the changing fortunes of a once formidable political power. Then there are the many towns that have recovered and reinvented themselves after wartime devastation, such as le Havre, as evocative as the bunkers and war museums of the D-Day beaches.

Whatever you search for, this large, varied and always surprising region is unlikely to disappoint.

Seine-Maritime and Eure

**Seine-Maritime stands apart from
the rest of the region. This
is a flat, windswept
country that rises
to a border of
white cliffs
along the Côte
d'Albâtre (Alabaster
Coast) and the Seine
Valley. Resorts and
harbour towns with
long seafaring histories
line the seaboard –
Dieppe, le Havre. Inland,
the Pays de Caux plateau
of Seine-Maritime is dotted
with aged farmhouses,
churches and châteaux, while
ancient beech woods gather alongside the Seine.**

Rouen

Farther up the river,
taking in part of the
Eure *département*,
lies the Normandie-
Vexin, a historic
administrative area
once bitterly fought
over by the medieval
kings of England and
France, and guarded
by strongholds such
as the mighty Château Gaillard (➤ 38–39). There is plenty to
explore here, but no trip to upper Normandy is complete without
a visit to its beautiful old capital, Rouen.

Rouen

Old and new Rouen oppose each other across the Seine: the new suburbs on the south bank, with their offices and tower blocks, and on the north bank a forest of Gothic spires. Venture into the old town and you encounter a fascinating world of medieval streets and busy alleyways overshadowed by the jettied gables of timber-framed houses and shops.

Celts and Romans had settlements here, and a church stood on the cathedral site by AD 393. When Rollo led his Viking invaders into Normandy he chose Rouen for his capital, and by the 12th

century it was being noted by a contemporary historian as a rich and pleasant town with 'great buildings, houses and churches'. A thriving weaving and textiles trade paid for more handsome buildings during the city's golden age, between the 15th and 17th centuries. After the disastrous bombardment of World War II many were painstakingly rebuilt, and today around 700 timber-framed houses survive. But Rouen is not a city with a uniform heritage. Some streets were spared the bombing and still have a shabby, precarious look, particularly along rue St-Vivien; there you will find unpolished, lived-in corners that have changed little over the centuries. There are also striking examples of later architecture, such as the railway station. Rouen has managed to retain its character without a stifling reverence; its fine churches, museums, historic buildings and many architectural surprises are all part of a vibrant, modern city, with one of the most attractive centres in France.

✚ 10D

Cathédrale Notre-Dame

A cathedral has stood on this site since the 4th century, though the earliest parts of the present building – apart from some 11th-century fragments – are 13th-century. Two very different towers flank the façade, giving it an eccentric yet attractive appeal. The Tour St-Romain, on the left as you face the cathedral, is crowned with a steep slate roof decorated with gold sunbursts. On the right is the ornate Tour de Beurre (Butter Tower), a 16th-century addition apparently funded by the sale of dispensations to Rouen's rich, allowing them to enjoy butter and milk during Lent. The 151m (495ft) central lantern tower, L'Aigle, with its cast-iron spire, was erected in 1876, replacing a 16th-century predecessor that had burned down.

Inside, beyond the soaring nave with its two-tiered arcades, the north transept contains a glorious 14th-century rose window and, rising from the balcony, the Escalier de la Librairie (Booksellers' Stairs). Traces of Roman columns can still be seen in the crypt, and effigies of Rollo, his son William Longsword, Henry, son of Henry II of England, and Richard the Lionheart are displayed in the ambulatory. The 14th-century Lady Chapel has two impressive tombs: one to the cardinals of Amboise, both called Georges, who are shown on their knees dressed in rich robes and framed by a Renaissance frieze; the other to Louis de Brézé whose wife, Diane de Poitiers, mistress of Henri II, is shown grieving over her husband.

✚ *Rouen 3c* ✉ 3 rue St-Romain ☎ 02 35 71 85 65 🕓 Apr–Oct Mon 2–7, Tue–Sat 7:30–7, Sun and public hols 8–6; Nov–Mar Mon 2–7, Tue–Sat 7:30–12, 2–6 🎟 Free 🚇 Palais de Justice 🚌 3, 13

Église St-Maclou

Badly damaged during World War II, this extravagant Flamboyant church finally reopened in 1980 after years of careful restoration. It was built between 1437 and 1517, dedicated to St Malo, a 7th-century missionary possibly of Welsh origin. Its wooden doors and stone porch are overwhelmed with carvings, some dating back to the 1550s, others decapitated deliberately. To the left of the porch a Renaissance fountain shows Bacchus flanked by two 'urinating' boys. Inside the church is a magnificent spiral staircase leading to the 16th-century organ case.

A short distance northeast from the church off rue Martainville is the Aître St-Maclou, a group of 16th-century timber-framed buildings around a courtyard. Originally the parish charnel-house, it is now part of the Fine Arts School. The galleries are decorated with macabre carvings of skeletons and skulls. Immediately right of the entrance, behind a glass panel, is the skeletal mummy of a cat.

✚ *Rouen 4c* ✉ Place Barthélemy ☎ 02 32 08 32 40 (Syndicat Initiative) 🕐 Mon–Sat 10–5, Sun 10:30–5:30. Aître courtyard daily 8–8 💷 Free 🚇 Palais de Justice 🚌 13

Musée des Antiquités

Housed in a 17th-century convent, this extensive collection includes Egyptian, Greek, Gallo-Roman and medieval artefacts, including its star exhibit, the famous 4th-century Mosaic of Lillebonne, the largest in France. Tapestries, tiles, Renaissance furniture and carved Rouennais façades are also on display. The natural history and ethnography museum is next door.

✚ *Rouen 3a* ✉ 198 rue Beauvoisine ☎ 02 35 98 55 10 🕐 Wed–Mon 10–12:15, 1:30–5:30, Sun 2–6 ✋ Inexpensive 🚇 Beauvoisine 🚌 6, 7, 20

Musée des Beaux-Arts

Paintings by Velázquez, Fragonard, Géricault, Caravaggio, David, Renoir and Monet are on view in this grand civic building that overlooks a small park and ornamental pond. The collection, spanning five centuries, takes in Russian icons, Impressionism and Raymond Duchamp-Villon's vigorous modern scuplture.

✚ *Rouen 2b* ✉ Esplanade Marcel Duchamp ☎ 02 35 71 28 40 🕐 Wed–Mon 10–6 ✋ Inexpensive 🚇 Palais de Justice ❓ A combined ticket allows admission to the Tour du Beffroi (➤ 54), Musée de la Céramique (➤ below) and Musée le Secq des Tournelles (➤ 86)

Musée de la Céramique

In the 17th and 18th centuries Rouen acquired fame and fortune producing faience, a style of tin-glazed earthenware with blue decoration on a white background or vice versa. Examples of this and other ceramics, including tableware and ornaments, are displayed in the 17th-century Hôtel d'Hocqueville, illustrating the industry's history.

✚ *Rouen 2b* ✉ 1 rue Faucon ☎ 02 35 07 31 74 🕐 Wed–Mon 10–1, 2–6 ✋ Inexpensive 🚇 Jeanne d'Arc 🚌 4, 11, 13, 20 ❓ A combined ticket allows admission to the Tour du Beffroi (➤ 54), Musée des Beaux-Arts (➤ above) and Musée le Secq des Tournelles (➤ 86)

Musée Flaubert et d'Histoire de la Médecine

This dual-purpose museum in the 18th-century Hôtel-Dieu has memorabilia of Gustave Flaubert in the room where he was born, and miscellaneous tools used in 19th-century hospitals. Exhibits include a childbirth demonstrator, surgical instruments and, for times when all else failed, statues of healing saints.

⊞ *Rouen 1c* ✉ 51 rue de Lecat ☎ 02 35 15 59 95 🕐 Tue 10–6, Wed–Sat 10–12, 2–6 ✋ Inexpensive 🚊 Boulevard des Belges 🚌 13

Musée le Secq des Tournelles

The 15th-century Église St-Laurent, all flying buttresses and tracery, is an apt setting for one of Rouen's most intriguing museums. On display is a collection of wrought ironwork in every imaginable form, from an elegant 18th-century banister (taken from the Château de Bellevue) to the loops and swirls of old shop signs, keys, door knockers and painful-looking corsets.

⊞ *Rouen 3b* ✉ 2 rue Jacques Villon ☎ 02 35 88 42 92 🕐 Wed–Sun 10–1, 2–6. Closed Tue and some hols 🚊 Palais de Justice 🚌 4, 11, 13, 20 ✋ Inexpensive ❓ A combined ticket allows admission to the Tour du Beffroi (► 54), Musée des Beaux-Arts (► 85) and Musée de la Céramique (► 85)

Palais de Justice

When Normandy was granted its own *parlement* in 1514 the city's new exchequer building and merchants' hall was chosen to house the debating chamber and law court. It certainly provided due pomp and decoration: pinnacles, gargoyles, statuettes and tracery cluster about the steep-pitched, grey roofs in a Gothic frenzy. Excavations in the palace courtyard uncovered the Monument Juif (Jewish Monument), the remains of a late 11th-century synagogue.

🕂 *Rouen 2c* ✉ 36 rue aux Juifs ☎ 02 35 88 55 88 🕒 Wed 2–6, Thu–Mon 10–6 ✋ Free 🚊 Palais de Justice 🚌 8

Rue du Gros-Horloge

Best places to see, pages 54–55.

Tour Jeanne d'Arc

Only a massive round donjon, with 4m-thick (13ft) walls and a witch's-hat roof, survives of the 13th-century fortress. The name is slightly misleading: Jeanne d'Arc (Joan of Arc) was imprisoned in another tower and was only brought here to be shown the torture chamber as part of the attempt to break her spirit. The tower now houses documents about Joan's trial along with displays tracing the history of the region.

🕂 *Rouen 2a* ✉ Rue Bouvreuil ☎ 02 35 98 16 21 🕒 Mon–Sat 10–12:30, 2–6:30 (until 5 Oct–Mar); Sun 2–6:30 (until 5 Oct–Mar) ✋ Inexpensive 🚊 Gare-rue-Verte 🚌 4, 11, 13, 20

a walk around old Rouen

This walk, starting at the cathedral, leads past some of the best architecture of the old town.

Turn right up rue St-Romain.

Medieval buildings are crammed along one side of the street; note Roussel's wrought-iron shopfront. At the archbishop's palace, opposite, Joan of Arc was condemned in 1431 and posthumously declared innocent 25 years later.

At place Barthélemy visit Église St-Maclou (▶ 84); then take rue Martainville and turn left at 186 for Aître St-Maclou (▶ 84). Return to place Barthélemy and turn right up rue Damiette. Continue to place du Lt-Aubert and detour left up rue d'Amiens.

Spectacular Rubenesque figures and other statues adorn the walls of the Medical Laboratory and the building opposite.

Return to the square and continue along rue des Boucheries-St-Ouen, then turn right up rue Eau-de-Robec, where footbridges cross a narrow stream.

On the right, housed in a splendid medieval building, the Musée de l'Éducation illustrates the upbringing and education of children.

Cross place St-Vivien and continue along rue Eau-de-Robec to rue Édouard-Adam. Turn left and head for place de la Croix de Pierre; then turn left up rue St-Vivien.

Beyond place St-Vivien, the street leads past Église St-Ouen, with its imposing and majestic vaulted ceilings, on the right, and a huddle of narrow timber-framed houses on the left.

Continue into rue de l'Hôpital and turn left on to rue des Carmes. Follow this to rue du Gros-Horloge. Turn right and continue under the Gros-Horloge (➤ 54) to place du Vieux-Marché, Rouen's old market square .

Distance About 2.5km (1.5 miles)
Time 1 hour, excluding visits
Start point Cathédrale Notre-Dame ✚ *Rouen 3c* 🚌 13
End point Place du Vieux-Marché ✚ *Rouen 1c* 🚌 8
Lunch La Taverne Walsheim (€€) ✉ Rue Martainville
☎ 02 35 98 27 50

More to see in Seine-Maritime and Eure

ABBAYE DU BEC-HELLOUIN

This walled Benedictine abbey in the tranquil Risle Valley was once a powerful religious, scholarly and political centre. The first two Norman archbishops of Canterbury, Lanfranc and Anselm, came from Bec; the abbey also produced many other influential churchmen, some of whom are listed on the 15th-century Tour St-Nicolas. In the new abbey church is the tomb of the anchorite Herluin, who founded the community in 1034; Lanfranc arrived eight years later having abandoned his teaching at Avranches. The monks fled during the French Revolution, but in 1948 a new community was re-established here – though not before the vast abbey church had been demolished (its foundations can still be seen opposite the tower, the only part to survive).

www.abbayedubec.com

✚ 9E ✉ 23km (14 miles) northeast of Bernay, on D130 ☎ 02 32 43 72 60 🕒 Self-guided tours Oct–May Wed–Mon 10:30, 3, 4, Sun and public hols 12, 3, 4; Jun–Sep Wed–Mon 10:30, 3, 4, 5, Sun and public hols 12, 3, 4 ✋ Moderate 🍴 Restaurants in village (€–€€€) 🚌 From Évreux ❓ Occasional concerts

ABBAYE DE JUMIÈGES

Best places to see, pages 36–37

ABBAYE DE ST-WANDRILLE

In 628 Count Wandrille renounced the secular world and after stops at various monasteries founded his own in the Seine Valley. It soon gained a reputation for scholarship but had to be rebuilt after Viking raids. The abbey passed into private hands after the French Revolution until 1931 when the Benedictine community

was re-established. Remains of the 14th-century abbey church and cloister can be seen in the grounds, as well as a 13th-century tithe barn rebuilt by the monks in 1967.

www.st-wandrille.com

✚ 9D ✉ 30km (18 miles) west of Rouen, off D982 ☎ 02 35 96 23 11 🕐 Guided tours of cloisters Wed–Mon 3:30, Sun 11:30, 3:30. Closed Mon, Easter Sun, 25 Dec
✋ Inexpensive (for tour) 🍴 Auberge Deux Couronnes (€€); tea rooms in village (€€) 🚌 From Rouen ❓ Visitors are asked not to talk loudly

LES ANDELYS AND CHÂTEAU GAILLARD

Best places to see, pages 38–39.

ARQUES-LA-BATAILLE

The donjon and walls of an 11th-century fortress dominate this riverside town. The battle referred to in the place name was in 1589, when Protestant Henri IV

saw off the superior forces of the Catholic League. Despite the siege and subsequent stone-robbing, the ruins are still impressive; the gatehouse shows a carved relief of the battle. Inside the town's 16th-century Église Notre-Dame de l'Assomption is a bust of Henri IV.

✚ 10B ☎ 02 32 14 40 60 🍴 Choice in Dieppe (€–€€€), or Manoir d'Archelles, south on D1 near Martigny (€–€€)
🚌 From Dieppe and Rouen

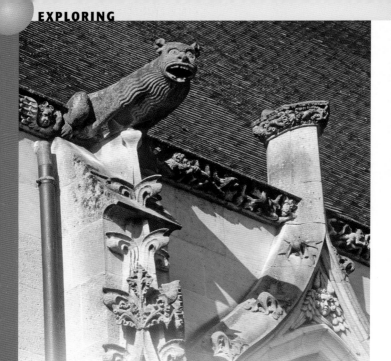

BEAUMONT-LE-ROGER

Situated on the edge of the Forêt de Beaumont, the walls of the priory ruins rise like a cliff from the roadside. Roger de Vieilles founded the Prieuré de la Sainte Trinité in 1070 near his castle, but the present remains are 13th-century. A steep path climbs under a series of arches to the hilltop ruins of the nave, with its wide eastern arch and a blind arcade along the length of the north wall. After the priory fell into disuse in the 1780s its relics were taken to the late medieval Église St-Nicolas near by.

www.beaumont-le-roger.fr

✚ 21H 🍴 Restaurants and cafés in town (€–€€) 🚌 From Évreux to Louviers; local buses from Louviers 🚆 From Évreux

BERNAY

Bernay's 11th-century abbey was founded by Judith of Brittany, wife of Duke Richard II, and its church still dominates this substantial country town where tributaries of the Charentonne wind among the streets. The interior of the early Romanesque church has carved capitals in the choir showing animals and foliage in the style of manuscript illuminations. Cars park opposite the apse, which is strikingly decorated with wooden tiles, and the abbey gardens lead to the **Musée des Beaux-Arts** in the former abbot's lodge, with its collection of art, sculpture and furniture. The town hall occupies the old abbey buildings beside the remains of the 13th-century cloisters. The Église Ste-Croix, on rue Alexandre, houses the tombstones of past abbots and of Guillaume d'Auvillars, a 15th-century abbot of le Bec-Hellouin.

✚ 20H ⑪ Restaurants, bars in town 🚌 From Pont-Audemer 🚉 From Lisieux, Évreux

Musée des Beaux-Arts

✉ Place Guillaume de Volpiano ☎ 02 32 46 63 23 🕐 Mid-Sep to mid-Jun Tue–Sun 2–5:30; mid-Jun to mid-Sep Tue–Sun 10–12, 2–7. Closed Mon, 1 Jan, 1 May, 25 Dec ✋ Inexpensive

BRIONNE

Brionne's importance as a strategic town goes back to the 11th century. Duke William laid siege to it between 1047 and 1050, eventually chasing out the duke of Burgundy. On a hill overlooking the town and the Risle Valley are the walls of a ruined 12th-century donjon. The slate-spired Église St-Martin dates mainly from the 15th century.

About 7km (4.5 miles) east of Brionne, an agricultural school occupies the moated Château d'Harcourt, set in extensive parkland and originally built for Robert of Harcourt, a companion of King Richard I of England.

✚ 9E ⑪ Restaurants and bars in town (€–€€) 🚌 From Évreux 🚉 From Rouen/Caen

BROGLIE

Broglie is a small rural town in the wooded Charentonne Valley. The 18th-century château (private) looms above the town on the site of an older fortress, and timber-framed houses crowd around the 12th-century Église St-Martin, built of contrasting conglomerate and limestone with later timber additions. Behind the church is an old leper house whose timbers are carved with dragons and the weathered face of a green man. Plaques commemorate two of Broglie's distinguished sons: Jean-François Merimée, born here in 1757 and later secretary of the École Nationale des Beaux-Arts; and civil engineer Augustin-Jean Fresnel, famous for his work in optics, born in 1788. A garden created on the marshy riverbank near the town centre displays willows, bamboo, ornamental rhubarb and other water-loving plants.

✚ 20H ⃓⃓ Restaurants and bars in town

CAUDEBEC-EN-CAUX

Extending along a wide stretch of the Seine, Caudebec has the air of a minor seaside resort, with shops and restaurants lining the waterfront. The Flamboyant Église Notre-Dame stands in the market place amid modern apartment blocks and shops. The Maison des Templiers, a 13th-century stone building, houses a local history display, and the Musée de la Marine de Seine looks at river navigation through the ages. Just outside the town the nose and wing of a stone biplane protrude from a rock, a memorial to five aviators who disappeared in the 1920s en route to the Arctic to rescue Italian balloonists who had crashed near Spitzbergen.

West of Caudebec, along the river, is the **Musée Départemental Victor Hugo,** where the writer's life is traced in his son-in-law's former home.

www.caudebec-en-caux.com

✚ 9D ⃓⃓ Restaurants (€€–€€€) ▣ From Rouen and le Havre

Musée Départemental Victor Hugo

🕐 Mon, Wed–Sat 10–12, 2–5:30 (6 in summer), Sun 2–5:30 or 6 🖐 Inexpensive

CHÂTEAU D'ANET

In 1531 the future King Henri II, then just 12 years old, fell under the spell of Diane de Poitiers, the beautiful 32-year-old widow of Louis de Brézé, former Lord of Anet. She became his mistress, and when Henri died in 1559 Diane retired to her château – a glorious showplace. Celebrated craftsmen worked here, including Benvenuto Cellini; Philibert Delorme designed the gateway and its extraordinary clock, with hounds that once barked the hour and a stag that stamped its hoof. Tours include the state rooms, and you can see the chapel and Diane's tomb (not guided).

www.chateaux-france.com

✚ 23J ☎ 02 37 41 90 07 🌐 Apr–Oct Wed–Mon 2–6:30; Nov, Feb–Mar Sat, Sun 2–6. Closed Dec, Jan ✋ Moderate
🍴 Restaurants in Anet (€–€€)
🚌 From Dreux

CHÂTEAU DE BEAUMESNIL

Behind the hamlet of Beaumesnil this 17th-century red-brick and stone château appears suddenly amid formal gardens, guarded by iron gates and railings. All that remains of the medieval fortress that once stood here is the overgrown base of its donjon. The later building has fashionable Flemish designs, and the grounds were laid out by La Quintinie, a student of André Le Nôtre. The interior contains a fine library, period furniture and a bookbinding museum.

www.chateaux-france.com

✚ 21H ✉ 13km (8 miles) southeast of Bernay by D140 ☎ 02 32 44 40 09
🕐 Jul–Aug Wed–Mon 11–6; Sep Wed–Mon 2–6; Easter–Jun Fri–Mon 2–6
✋ Moderate 🍴 L'Etape Louis XIII (€€–€€€), in village

CHÂTEAU DU CHAMP-DE-BATAILLE

This grand red-brick and stone château stands in a flat, open landscape ringed with woodland, and retains the atmosphere of an aristocratic country house. Part of the building is used as a golf club – the course is laid out within the grounds – but the main

rooms are open to the public and include the duchess's bedroom, the billiard room, hung with tapestries, and a hall decorated with carvings representing the four seasons.

www.chateauduchampdebataille.com

🕀 9E ☎ 02 32 34 84 34 🕐 Easter–All Saints' Day daily 2–6; Jun–Aug daily 10–6 🧑 Expensive 🍽 Restaurant (€€) 🚌 From Évreux

CHÂTEAU DE MARTAINVILLE

Privateer Jacques le Pelletier built this château in the late 15th century, and his nephew later transformed it from a fortified house into a stately home. Its round, red-brick towers are topped with conical roofs and there is a large 16th-century dovecote in the grounds. Inside is the Musée Départemental des Traditions et Arts Normands, with a collection of furniture, ceramics, glass and costumes.

🕀 11D ✉ 16km (10 miles) east of Rouen ☎ 02 35 23 44 70 🕐 Wed–Mon 10–12:30, 2–6:30 (till 6 in winter). Closed Tue and Sun am 🧑 Inexpensive 🍽 Restaurants in village (€€) 🚌 From Rouen

CHÂTEAU DE MIROMESNIL

Guy de Maupassant (1850–93) was born in this 16th-century red-brick and stone château. Memorabilia associated with the writer are displayed inside, as well as books collected by the Marquis de Miromesnil, Louis XVI's chancellor, who died here in 1796. A 16th-century chapel with an ornate interior stands in the grounds.

www.chateaumiromesnil.com

🚩 10B 🖂 Tourville-sur-Arques
☎ 02 35 85 02 80 🕐 1 Apr–1 Nov daily 2–6 🖐 Moderate 🚌 From Dieppe (summer)

CLÈRES

A large covered market hall forms the centre of this quiet village, but the main attraction lies to the west where the 19th-century neo-Gothic Château de Clères stands on the site of an 11th-century stronghold. Since 1920 its grounds have been given over to the **Parc Zoologique** whose inhabitants include flamingos, emus, peacocks, kangaroos and antelopes. At nearby Montville, the **Musée**

des Sapeurs-Pompiers has a collection of vintage fire engines, plus uniforms and documents relating to the fire service.

🕂 10C 🍴 Choice of restaurants (€–€€)
🚌 From Rouen

Parc Zoologique
☎ 02 35 33 23 08 🕐 Mar–Sep daily 10–7; Oct 9–12, 1:30–5 ✋ Inexpensive

Musée des Sapeurs-Pompiers
☎ 02 35 33 13 51; www.musee-sapeurs-pompiers.org 🕐 Apr–Oct daily 1–6; Nov–Mar weekends 1–6

CONCHES-EN-OUCHE

Conches lies on the edge of yet another ancient Norman territory, the Pays d'Ouche, with views of the Forêt de Conches to the west, and from the medieval château the lush Rouloir Valley to the east. The château ruins consist of a circular donjon and overgrown towers, all grouped on a motte and set in a small public garden. Near by, the Église Ste-Foy has an elaborate iron spire and carved 16th-century door. Both fortress and church are associated with the lords of Tosny: the former was built by them in the 12th century and the latter occupies the site of a church founded in the 11th century by Roger de Tosny, who returned from a pilgrimage bearing relics of Sainte Foy.

Local artist François Décorchement (1880–1971) is celebrated in the **Musée du Verre et de la Pierre,** which displays three of his stained-glass windows and has superb exhibitions of modern glasswork.

www.conches-en-ouche.fr

🕂 21H 🍴 Choice of restaurants (€–€€) 🚌 From Évreux 🚉 From Évreux

Musée du Verre et de la Pierre
✉ Route de Sainte-Marguerite ☎ 02 32 30 90 41 🕐 Mid-Mar to Nov Wed–Sat 2–5:30 ✋ Inexpensive

DIEPPE
Best places to see, pages 44–45.

ECOUIS

Planted incongruously in the middle of this unremarkable village is the twin-towered collegiate church of Notre-Dame, visible from afar across the flat countryside. Built in the early 14th century by King Philip IV's finance minister, Enguerrand de Marigny, it has a wonderfully spacious interior lit by two large stained-glass transept windows. Look out for the brick vault and intricately carved bosses in the side chapel, carved doors and wooden ceiling in the enclosed chapel near the entrance, and timber spiral stairs leading to the organ loft.
www.collegiale-ecouis.asso.fr
✚ 11E 🍴 None in village

ÉTRETAT
Étretat is the most attractive Norman resort north of Honfleur and is always busy in summer. Out of season it carries on a quiet but cheerful life of its own. The shingle beach stretches between two

glaring chalk headlands, both sculpted by the elements. The Falaise d'Aval (western cliff) ends in a wide and fragile-looking arch, a flying buttress against the main body of rock. The eastern cliff, the Falaise d'Amont, is less dramatic. Perched on top of it is the seamen's chapel of Notre-Dame-de-la-Garde, and a monument commemorating Charles Nungesser and François Coli, French aviators who set out from Paris in 1927 to try and cross the Atlantic to New York in their plane 'Oiseau Blanc'; they were last seen over this part of the coast. There is also a museum with mementoes of the pilots.

The centre of the town is full of character. In place du Maréchal Foch 16th-century town houses are grouped around the wooden *halles* (covered market), where in summer souvenir shops open under the first-floor galleries; over the entrance to the *halles* is an unusual carving of a bat with a man's head. A plaque beneath the clock tower in the *place* commemorates Étretat's World War I field hospital, and the arrival of Scottish troops in World War II.

www.etretat.net

✚ 8C 🍴 Choice of restaurants (€–€€€)

along the Côte d'Albâtre

a drive

This coastal drive detours inland to explore the Pays de Caux.

From Dieppe take the D75 signed St-Valéry-en-Caux.

The road twists down into the breezy resort of Pourville-sur-Mer, with panoramic sea views.

Continue along the D75 through Varengeville-sur-Mer (▶ 112) to Ste-Marguerite-sur-Mer.

Stop here to look at the 12th- to 16th-century church. To the right of the entrance is a carving of an owl holding a snake in its beak; owl motifs are repeated on columns in the dark interior.

At St-Aubin-sur-Mer follow the coast to Veules-les-Roses; turn right on to the D925 (St-Valéry-en-Caux). Take the D925 towards Fécamp and turn on to the D68 (signed St-Sylvain). The road passes through a broad, flat landscape with an aerodrome in the distance, before descending through beech woods into Paluel. Continue to St-Martin-aux-Buneaux and take the D68 to Sassetot-le-Mauconduit.

At Malleville-les-Grès, beyond Paluel, the D68 passes a handsome manor house and a 1650 stone cross. Next, a turreted wall surrounds the lordly 15th-century château at Auberville-la-Manuel. Facing the road at Sassetot is a pink and white château, now a hotel.

Follow signs to Valmont (▶ 112). Take the D150 to Fécamp (▶ 106), then the D940 and D104 to Yport.From Yport, with its impressive red-brick and

limestone church, the D211 winds through woodland, overlooking the sea, to Vattetot-sur-Mer. At Vattetot turn right on to the D11 and descend into a green valley on the approach to Étretat.

Distance 80km (50 miles)
Time 2.5 hours, excluding visits
Start point Dieppe ✚ 10B
End point Étretat ✚ 8C
Lunch Le Relais des Dalles (€€) ✉ 6 rue Elisabeth d'Autriche, Sassetot-la-Mauconduit ☎ 02 35 27 41 83

EU

Set on the Bresle river, with the Forêt d'Eu spreading towards the southeast, this once powerful *ville royale* has two buildings out of proportion to the small centre. The grandiose red-brick and stone Château d'Eu, on the site of an older fortress where William the Conqueror was married, was the favoured home of King Louis-Philippe and houses the **Musée Louis-Philippe,** where porcelain, paintings and ornate furniture are on display in the salons. Facing it is the medieval Église Notre-Dame et St-Laurent, which houses the remains of Saint Laurence O'Toole, a 12th-century archbishop of Dublin.

www.ville-eu.fr

🚑 11A 🍴 Hôtel Restaurant Mairie, 20 avenue de la Gare (€–€€)

🚌 From Rouen/Dieppe

Musée Louis-Philippe

☎ 02 35 86 44 00 🕐 Mid-Mar to early Nov Wed–Mon 10–12, 2–6 (Fri pm only) 🖐 Inexpensive

ÉVREUX

The ancient capital of the Eure, on the banks of the Iton, has been rebuilt many times following invasion, siege and war, yet still preserves some notable historic monuments and an attractive centre. A riverside walk leads from the restored 12th- to 17th-century Cathédrale Notre-Dame to the Tour de l'Horloge, a free-standing tower built in 1490. The tower's bell strikes the hour.

Évreux's turbulent history is traced in the Musée de l'Ancien Évêché, next to the cathedral, housed in the former 15th-century bishop's palace. Grouped around the central place Charles de Gaulle are the elegant 19th-century Hôtel Dieu, Maison des Arts, theatre, and the library with its startling modern annexe in the form of a wooden bowl. West of the centre lies the 12th-century Église St-Taurin; the one-time abbey church contains a fine 13th-century reliquary, gold-plated with enamelled silver, that contains the relics of Saint Taurin.

www.ot-pays-evreux.fr

🚑 22H 🍴 Choice of restaurants (€–€€€) 🚌 From Rouen and Honfleur

🚂 From Cherbourg

FÉCAMP

This workaday harbour town is the home of Bénédictine liqueur, made from a secret recipe discovered by Alexandre le Grand in a 16th-century monastic manuscript. Le Grand promoted the product with gusto, commissioning posters by celebrated artists and building the neo-Gothic **Palais Bénédictine.** This now contains an art gallery and museum, as well as the copper Bénédictine stills; tours and tastings are provided.

For centuries Fécamp was a major centre of pilgrimage and people flocked to the monastery to see the relic of the Precious Blood of Christ; it was supposedly washed ashore in a hollow fig tree and is now housed in the Église de La Trinité.

www.fecamptourisme.com

✚ 8C 🍴 Choice of restaurants on quays (€–€€) 🚌 From Dieppe, Rouen
🚊 From Rouen

Palais Bénédictine

✉ 110 rue Alexandre-le-Grand ☎ 02 35 10 26 10 🕐 Feb–Mar, mid-Oct to Dec daily 10:30–11:45, 2–6; Apr to mid-Jul, Sep, Oct daily 10–1, 2–6:30; mid-Jul to Aug daily 10–7 ✋ Moderate

GISORS

The capital of the Normandie-Vexin stands on rising ground beside the region's eastern border, amid seemingly endless flatlands. Behind the main street are the ruins of a 12th-century fortress, where a slender donjon was built by King Henry II of England; it is surrounded by moss-covered walls and a filled-in ditch where locals now play *boules*. King Philippe Auguste added the Tour du Prisonnier, which became a prison in the 16th century – drawings and inscriptions by the inmates can still be seen. Across town the church of St-Gervais et St-Protais contains an impressive Tree of Jesse.

www.ville-gisors.fr

✚ 12E 🍴 Choice of restaurants (€€–€€€) 🚌 From Évreux

GIVERNY

Visitors come to this riverside hamlet to see Claude Monet's house and the gardens that he created and later painted. Footpaths lead round the gardens, which are very beautiful but inevitably obscured by the crowds. The most popular photo opportunity is the water-lily pond and its bridge, familiar from Monet's famous series of paintings. A road through the **Jardins Monet** divides the Clos Normand (enclosed garden) from the Water Garden. The artist's 'pink house' has reproductions of his works, Japanese engravings, and rooms decorated in different colours. The Musée d'Art Américain, near by, celebrates the works of American artists past and present.

www.giverny.org

🕀 23H 🍴 Terra Café at Musée d'Art Américain (€€). Closed Feb 🚌 From Vernon station (spring–autumn)

Jardins Monet

✉ On the D5 ☎ 02 32 51 28 21 🕐 Apr–Oct Tue–Sun 9:30–6. Also Easter and Whit Monday 👢 Moderate

LE HAVRE

From the Pont de Normandie and the east, traffic enters le Havre past petrochemical factories into a maze of low apartment blocks and shops. This is the modern centre designed by Auguste Perret after the old town was levelled in World War II. One of the few pre-war survivors is the 17th-century building housing the Musée de l'Ancien Havre, a token of the town's

former character (may be temporarily closed for building works).

Le Havre has a long seafaring pedigree, but rather than try to recapture the past Perret went for unapologetic modernism. Beyond the *bassin du commerce* (commercial dock), crossed by an elegant white bridge, a ship's funnel rises from the underground bowl of

Espace Oscar Niemeyer, home of Le Volcan arts centre. Inside Perret's monumental Église St-Joseph to the west, light sparkles through the stained glass of the 109m (358ft) octagonal lantern tower. To the south, the 16th-century Cathédrale Notre-Dame is an eccentric mix of architectural styles.

www.lehavretourisme.com

➕ 7D 🍴 Restaurants in Ste-Adresse area (€€–€€€) 🚌 From Caen, Lisieux and Caudebec-en-Caux (connection with Rouen) 🚉 From Rouen

LYONS-LA-FORÊT

Huddled in a dip of the Lieure Valley, Lyons-la-Forêt is a classic Norman timber-framed village, where narrow 17th-century buildings crowd round the old *halles*. These houses and the 12th-century Église St-Denis are the only sights as such, but the prettiness of this picture-postcard village makes it a popular choice as a base for exploring the surrounding Forêt de Lyons.

Among the slender beeches – which filter an ethereal light even into the heart of the forest – is the Abbaye de Mortemer, ruins of a medieval Cistercian abbey with a museum of monastic life. Here also are the Château de Fleury-la-Forêt with its collection of toys and dolls, and the **Château de Vascœuil** on the forest's edge, with reconstructions of traditional cottages in its grounds, with a sculpture path and contemporary art exhibits.

www.lyons.tourisme.free.fr

✚ 11D 🍴 La Licorne (€€–€€€)

🚌 From Rouen

Château de Vascoeuil

☎ 02 35 23 62 35;
www.chateauvascoeuil.com ⬛ Mid-Mar to mid-Nov Tue–Sun 2:30–6:30; Jul, Aug daily 11–7 ✋ Moderate 🍴 Restaurant La Cascade (€€), in the château

PONT-AUDEMER

Pont-Audemer's prosperity was built on its tanneries, and it retains the air of a working town. Situated between two branches of the Risle river, it is known as the Little Venice of Normandy. The modern shops and houses blend with narrow alleyways and courtyards lined with historic buildings. Canals cut through town, crossed by small wooden footbridges, and there are good examples of 17th-century housing along rue de la République, Cour Canel and near the 11th-century Église St-Ouen.

✚ 8D 🍴 Choice of cafés and restaurants (€–€€) 🚌 From Lisieux or Rouen

ST-MARTIN-DE-BOSCHERVILLE

This tiny village is dominated by the former abbey church, now the parish church of St-Georges-de-Boscherville. Refounded as a Benedictine monastery in 1144, it housed a small community of monks until they fled during the Revolution. Wide steps ascend to the church's simple Romanesque façade, built of gleaming limestone with a fine doorway. Inside, the space and light created by its austere design is breathtaking; look for the puppet-like carvings on the transept columns.

www.abbaye-saint-georges.com

✚ 10D ✉ 10km (6 miles) northwest of Rouen off D982 ☎ 02 35 32 10 82
✋ Inexpensive 🍴 Bars near the church (€) 🚌 From Rouen

LE TRÉPORT

The bracing seaside resort of le Tréport lies on the region's windswept northeastern corner. High chalk cliffs shelter a shingle beach and provide views from the Calvaire des Terrasses. The restored 16th-century Église St-Jacques at the end of quai François 1er overlooks the harbour and fishing boats; its 11th-century predecessor disappeared with former cliffs into the sea.

www.ville-le-treport.fr

✚ 11A 🍴 Choice of cafés and seafood restaurants along quai François 1er
(€€) 🚌 From Rouen and Dieppe

VALMONT

From the flint and brick church at the centre of this small country town you can look up at the high, buttressed walls and slate roofs of the château established by the powerful Estouteville family. In 1169 Nicolas d'Estouteville founded the Benedictine **abbey** whose ruins stand at the foot of a wooded slope. They include the 16th-century choir, and the graceful Chapelle de la Vierge, or Six Heures (the time of the daily mass), that houses the tombs of Jacques d'Estouteville and the abbey's founder; five 15th-century windows depict the life of the Virgin.

➕ 8C 🍴 Auberge du Bec au Cauchois, (€–€€) 🚌 From Rouen

Abbaye

☎ 02 35 27 34 92 🕐 Guided tours: Apr–Sep Wed–Mon 2–5 ✋ Free

VARENGEVILLE-SUR-MER

The wooded coast road runs southwest of Dieppe through a series of townships that make up Varengeville. Just inland the privateer-politician Jean Ango built his summer palace, the **Manoir d'Ango,** in the 1530s, decorating it with busts of the great and good, including François I and himself.

Closer to the coast, the gardens of the **Parc Floral du Bois des Moutiers** include rhododendrons and magnolias among the shrubs offering spring colour. Formal flower beds are arranged around a house built in 1898 from the designs of the English architect Edwin Lutyens. In the town's cliff-top church is a stunning stained-glass Tree of Jesse by Georges Braque; the cubist painter came to live here in 1930.

➕ 10B 🍴 Hôtel de la Terrasse (€–€€) 🚌 From Dieppe

Manoir d'Ango

✉ 7km (4 miles) west of Dieppe ☎ 02 35 85 14 80 🕐 Mar–Nov Tue–Sun and public hols 10–12:30, 2–6:30 ✋ Moderate

Parc Floral du Bois des Moutiers

✉ 78km (48 miles) west of Dieppe ☎ 02 35 85 10 02 🕐 Mid-Mar to mid-Nov daily 10–12, 2–6 ✋ Moderate

VERNEUIL-SUR-AVRE

Historic Verneuil is composed of three precincts. Each was once protected by a series of moated walls, and you can still walk along part of the outer moat, which enclosed the whole town.
The grim, windowless Tour Grise, built by Philippe Auguste after the French had taken the town in 1204, is a circular donjon similar to the Tour

Jeanne d'Arc in Rouen (➤ 87). The town suffered further during the Hundred Years War due to its position on the border between French and English territory. Timber-framed and stone buildings crowd around the Église de la Madeleine, a 12th-century church whose later, Flamboyant tower is crowned with an elegant filigree lantern. The Église Notre-Dame has 16th-century statuary by local sculptors.

www.verneuilsuravre.com

✚ 21J 🍴 Restaurants and bars in town (€–€€€) 🚌 From Évreux

VERNON

Vernon is a bustling market town on the Seine. Many of its medieval buildings survive, one of the best, with faded 15th-century carvings, housing the tourist office on rue Carnot; the nearby Gothic church has striking abstract stained-glass windows. The massive circular donjon visible from the rue du Vieux Château was once part of the castle built by King Philippe Auguste. Across the river, near the miniature Château des Tourelles, a timber-framed house perches on a stump of the former medieval bridge.

The **Musée Alphonse-Georges Poulain** features paintings by Manet and Bonnard, as well as exhibits relating to the area's archaeology and history.

Just outside Vernon the 18th-century **Château de Bizy**, set in terraced gardens, has a fine collection of tapestries.

✚ 23H 🍴 Restaurants (€–€€€) 🚌 From Évreux

Musée Alphonse-Georges Poulain

✉ 12 rue du Pont ☎ 02 32 21 28 09 🕐 Apr–Sep Tue–Fri 10:30–12:30, 2–6, Sat, Sun 2–6; Oct–Mar Tue–Sun 2–5:30

Château de Bizy

✉ 2km (1.2 miles) south of Vernon ☎ 02 32 51 00 82 🕐 Apr–Oct Tue–Sun 10–12, 2–6; Mar weekends 2–5. Closed Nov–Feb 👆 Moderate

HOTELS

LES ANDELYS
Hôtel de Paris (€€)
A handsome, red-brick 19th-century building on the approach road into Grand Andely, with a restaurant.
✉ 10 avenue de la République ☎ 02 32 54 00 33

CAUDEBEC-EN-CAUX
Le Cheval Blanc (€€)
Charming Logis de France hotel by the Seine on the abbeys' circuit. Friendly welcome and pleasant restaurant.
✉ Place René Coty ☎ 02 35 96 21 66 🕔 Closed 15 Feb–9 Mar

CLÈRES
Véronique Degonse Chambres d'Hôtes (€€)
Bed and breakfast in one double room, in Véronique Degonse's turn-of-the-20th-century home surrounded by wooded grounds.
✉ 76690 Clères ☎ 02 35 33 34 38

ÉTRETAT
Domaine St Clair (€€–€€€)
Swim year round in the heated outdoor pool, where you can gaze up at the ivy covered turrets of this impressive hotel. Splash out on a four-poster bed and magnificent views or settle for something more modest, but still comfortable, in this château-hotel. Ideal for special occasions or pampering indulgence.
✉ Chemin de St Clair ☎ 02 35 27 08 23

L'Escale (€–€€)
A no-frills hotel, which represents great value. Attractive rooms and a small restaurant serving simple meals. Sea views.
✉ Place Foch ☎ 02 35 27 03 69

EU
Domaine de Joinville (€€€)
One for special occasions, a château/hotel with a pool, gardens and fitness centre offering massage and other treatments. Rooms

are expensive but the restaurant has reasonably priced options. Meals can be eaten outside on the terrace.

✉ Route du Tréport, 1km (0.5 miles) west ☎ 02 35 50 52 52

ÉVREUX
France (€€)
See page 74.

GISORS
Hostellerie des Trois Poissons (€€)
Impressive timber-framed building on the lively main street, between the church and the château.

✉ 13 rue Cappeville ☎ 02 32 55 01 09 🕐 Summer (except last half of Jun) until end Oct

LE HAVRE
Clarine Hôtel-Restaurant (€€)
A sprawling glass building near the main road and harbour, with a McDonald's next door. Rooms offer good facilities and convenience for travellers.

✉ Quai Colbert ☎ 02 35 26 49 49

ROUEN
Le Bristol (€€)
Overlooking the Palais de Justice and near the rue du Gros-Horloge. Comfortable rooms and parking – a great asset in this largely pedestrianized part of town.

✉ 45 rue aux Juifs ☎ 02 35 71 54 21

Citotel le Viking d'Angleterre (€€)
A good bet for an overnight stay. Set on a busy riverside road, but rooms at the rear, overlooking the bus station, are much quieter. Small, clean and convenient rooms with all the basics.

✉ 21 quai du Havre ☎ 02 35 70 34 95

Hôtel de la Cathédrale (€€–€€€)
See page 74.

Hôtel de Dieppe (€€–€€€)

As you would expect from a Best Western hotel, you get all the mod cons, but there's also a highly reputable restaurant, Le Quatre Saisons.

✉ Place B Tissot ☎ 02 35 71 96 00

LE TRÉPORT
Le Saint-Yves (€–€€)

A friendly, traditional resort hotel with flowery decor and a restaurant serving good-value seafood.

✉ 7 quai Albert Cauët ☎ 02 35 86 34 66

RESTAURANTS

BRIONNE
Auberge du Vieux Donjon (€€)

Excellent restaurant-with-rooms in an 18th-century inn on the main street of the village. Prettily decorated with flowers and warmed by a real fire. The menu includes superb seafood.

✉ 19 rue de la Soie ☎ 02 32 44 80 62 🕔 Lunch, dinner. Closed Mon, Sun eve, Thu eve in winter

CAUDEBEC-EN-CAUX
Le Cheval Blanc (€–€€)

This family-run hotel restaurant offers value for money. Truly authentic Normandy cuisine with favourites such as foie gras and Vire Andouille sausages on the menu.

✉ Place René Coty ☎ 02 35 96 21 66 🕔 Lunch, dinner. Closed 15 Feb– 9 Mar, Fri, Sat lunch, Sun eve

DIEPPE
L'Armorique (€–€€)

A first-floor restaurant and ground-floor café attached to a fish shop, overlooking the fishing boats. *Assiettes de fruits de mer* come in two sizes, enormous and unbelievable. The menu ranges from simple and cheap to sophisticated and slightly pricier.

✉ 17 quai Henri IV ☎ 02 35 84 28 14 🕔 Lunch, dinner. Closed Sun eve, Mon

Marmite Dieppoise (€€)

Located near the harbour, this popular seafood restaurant serves the local speciality of bowls heaped with a variety of shellfish.

✉ 8 rue St-Jean ☎ 02 35 84 24 26 🕒 Lunch, dinner. Closed mid-Nov to mid-Dec, late Feb to mid-Mar, Thu in winter, Sun eve, Mon

ÉTRETAT
L'Huitrière (€€–€€€)

A conspicuous semicircular building under the Falaise d'Aval, housing a restaurant on two floors with panoramic sea views. Seafood is the speciality, and comes in enormous quantities.

✉ Place du Général de Gaulle ☎ 02 35 27 02 82 🕒 Lunch, dinner

Les Roches Blanches (€–€€)

See page 59.

ÉVREUX
Camomille (€€)

See page 58.

Restaurant Michel Thomas (€–€€)

Norman specialities with an individual touch – duck, veal, and inventive desserts such as spicy fruit puddings. Served in a smart, quiet building on a busy shopping street.

✉ 87 rue Joséphine ☎ 02 32 33 05 70 🕒 Lunch, dinner. Closed Sun

La Sarrazine (€)

You need to reserve a table at this very popular crêperie. The food is superb and the cider flows all evening.

✉ 4 rue des Lombards ☎ 02 32 33 04 60 ✉ Lunch, dinner. Closed Mon, Sun lunch

LYONS-LA-FORÊT
La Licorne (€€–€€€)

A restaurant with comfortable rooms in a beautiful old pink-and-brown timber-framed building overlooking the historic market hall. Popular and reliable.

✉ Place Bensérade ☎ 02 32 49 62 02 🕐 Lunch, dinner. Closed mid-Dec to mid-Jan, Sun eve, Mon in winter

ROUEN
Al Dente (€)
A respite from the city's fine cuts of meat and creamy cheeses. Choose a perfectly cooked pasta dish as a lighter option for both the wallet and the waistline. An unexpected treat in an old half-timbered house.
✉ 24 rue Cauchoise ☎ 02 35 70 24 25 🕐 Lunch, dinner

Le Beffroy (€€)
Straightforward local cooking using cider; good seafood and a choice of game. The setting is a very old building in a quiet street; the atmosphere is smart but animated. A popular choice.
✉ 15 rue Beffroy ☎ 02 35 71 55 27 🕐 Lunch, dinner. Closed Tue, Sun eve

La Couronne (€€–€€€)
Set in a 14th-century Norman building, this famous restaurant in the historic heart of Rouen claims to be the oldest not only in the city but in France. Gourmets are prepared to pay for the excellent food, but it is possible to sample it at slightly lower prices.
✉ 31 place du Vieux-Marché ☎ 02 35 71 40 90 🕐 Lunch, dinner

Écaille (€€€)
A classy restaurant, serving delicacies such as lobster salad with ingenious combinations of ingredients. Calvados naturally makes an appearance. One of Rouen's finest seafood restaurants.
✉ 26 rampe Cauchoise ☎ 02 35 70 95 52 🕐 Lunch, dinner. Closed Sat lunch and Sun eve, Mon, 1 week in Aug (varies)

Les Garamantes (€€)
Traditional Norman dishes of the old days have been supplanted by fashionable Libyan specialities: couscous and *Tajines*. Eat in or choose takeaway for an exotic picnic.
✉ 4 rue Ste-Croix-des-Pelletiers ☎ 02 35 70 56 83 🕐 Lunch, dinner

Gill (€€€)

Rouennais meals are given a modern touch in this cool, green, modern building by the Seine. Lobster and pigeon are among the offerings; an experience as well as a good meal.

✉ 8–9 quai de la Bourse ☎ 02 35 71 16 14 🕔 Lunch, dinner. Closed Aug, Sun, Mon

Le Maupassant (€–€€)

Hidden among the tourist traps on the square by the Joan of Arc church is this lively choice of the younger locals. Dazzling with mirrors and heavily hung with theatrical drapes, this glamorous bistro is perfect for unwinding after a hard day's shopping.

✉ 39 place du Vieux Marché ☎ 02 35 07 56 90 🕔 Lunch, dinner. Closed Sun

Nature (€–€€)

A pleasant vegetarian option near the cathedral, serving healthy lunches from a counter in the corner of a health-food shop.

✉ 3 rue Petit Salut ☎ 02 35 98 15 74 🕔 Tue–Sat 12–2. Closed Sun, Mon

L'Orangerie (€–€€)

An atmospheric, vaulted room and courtyard with plants, statues and a cheerful, comfortable feel. Tables are set outside in spring and summer, and the reasonable menu includes good seafood.

✉ 2 rue Thomas Corneille ☎ 02 35 88 43 97 🕔 Lunch, dinner

Le Temps des Cerises (€–€€€)

The title may say cherries, but the menu shouts of local apples and cheeses. Enjoy the best of Normandy's dairies and orchards and experiment with cheesy *raclettes* and fondues from across France.

✉ 4–6 rue des Basnages ☎ 02 35 89 98 00 🕔 Closed Sat–Mon lunch

LE TRÉPORT

Le Homard Bleu (€–€€)

One of a huge choice of seafood restaurants along the harbour quay, offering cheaper weekday menus.

✉ 45 quai François 1er ☎ 02 35 86 15 89 🕔 Lunch, dinner. Closed Jan to mid-Feb

VILLEQUIER
Grand Sapin (€–€€)

Atmospheric hotel-restaurant with period furniture and balconies overlooking the Seine. Traditional dishes and seafood, using local ingredients. Wood-panelled dining room.

✉ 12 rue Louis le Graffic ☎ 02 35 56 78 73 🕐 Lunch, dinner. Closed late Nov, mid-Feb to mid-Mar, Tue eve, Wed Sep–Jun

SHOPPING

FASHION
Catimini

Pretty children's clothes in eye-catching colours and designs; also shoes and accessories.

✉ 50 rue des Carmes, Rouen ☎ 02 35 07 18 00

Florence Kooijman

A shoe designer who also has outlets in Lille, le Touquet and Amiens. Elegant shoes and ankle boots in suede or leather at reasonable prices.

✉ 11 rue Ganterie, Rouen ☎ 02 35 89 35 81

Gary Bis

Smart contemporary menswear, at a price. A hint of Parisian style.

✉ 6–8 rue Eugène Boudin, Rouen ☎ 02 35 71 96 53

FOOD
Chocolaterie Auzou

This master chocolate maker in the city centre is an essential detour on any walking tour. Delicious hand-made creations to make your mouth water. Also branches in Évreux and le Havre.

✉ 163 rue du Gros-Horloge, Rouen ☎ 02 35 70 59 31

Héloin Anne-Marie

Delicious sweets, chocolates and other goodies such as *pains d'épices* (gingerbread), jams, marmalades and honey, all beautifully presented.

✉ 98 rue des Carmes, Rouen ☎ 02 35 71 02 94

La Valeine

Home-made ice cream, cider and goats' cheese from this farm shop on the edge of town.

✉ Manoir de Cateuil, route du Havre, Évreux ☎ 02 35 27 14 02

GIFTS
Antiquité Boisnard

This antique shop is almost 100 years old and is an old favourite for choosing that special present.

✉ 54 rue République, Rouen ☎ 02 35 70 60 08

Carpentier Faïencier

The famous blue and white *faïences de Rouen*, once de rigeur at the French court, make excellent presents and stylish souvenirs. This shop and workshop has several unique pieces made on site.

✉ 26 rue St-Romain, Rouen ☎ 02 35 88 77 47

La Galerie Montador

Art gallery and children's gift and toy shop, with wooden trains, puppets and bricks, Tintin T-shirts, and grown-ups' gifts such as lamps and ship-shape condiments.

✉ 4 rue Bains, Dieppe ☎ 02 35 82 63 03

Ma Normandie

In the heart of the old town, specializing in faience (decorated ceramics) in the form of ornaments, pots and plates. Other gifts include pictures and barometers.

✉ 48 rue St-Nicolas, Rouen ☎ 02 35 71 46 08

Les Perles de Charlotte

Charlotte Le Goff's original jewellery, from bracelets to brooches, is sold in the workshop boutique.

✉ 9 rue Alphonse Karr, Étretat ☎ 06 17 71 53 70

Tentations

Painted wooden ornaments, jewellery, umbrellas and other gifts.

✉ Rue Docteur Oursel, Évreux ☎ 02 32 31 66 65

ENTERTAINMENT

LIVE MUSIC VENUES

L'Hermès
New bands and retro gigs in this stalwart of the port music scene.
✉ 348 avenue Aristide Briand, le Havre ☎ 02 35 24 35 84

McDaid's
An Irish theme pub that sells Guinness, has a pool table, and
features folk, rock and jazz bands on Thursdays and Fridays.
✉ 97 rue Paul Doumer, le Havre ☎ 02 35 41 30 40 🕐 2pm–2am

Le Saxo
Late-night bar with regular jazz nights and an eclectic clientele.
✉ 11 place Saint-Marc, Rouen ☎ 02 35 98 24 92

THEATRES AND CONCERT HALLS

La Chapelle St Louis
This venue takes in touring national and international productions
as well as showcasing student and fringe groups from the city.
✉ Place de la Rougemare, Rouen ☎ 02 35 98 45 05

Opera de Rouen
Major operatic and ballet productions, plus classical concerts,
staged in a modern building overlooking the Seine.
✉ 7 rue du Docteur Rambert, Rouen ☎ 02 35 71 41 36

Théâtre des Bains Douches
An interesting range of contemporary and experimental drama
productions, as well as some fringe music events.
✉ 22 rue Louis Lobasso, le Havre ☎ 02 35 47 63 09

Théâtre de l'Hôtel de Ville
Popular productions and family shows in an annexe of the city's
modern town hall, overlooking the central square's lawns and
fountains.
✉ Place de l'Hôtel de Ville, le Havre ☎ 02 35 19 45 45

Calvados and Orne

Caen

**Central Normandy
is composed of a variety
of landscapes, from the
D-Day beaches and
seaside resorts of the
Côte Fleurie and the Côte de Nacre, to
the quiet towns of the rural south.**

Between the coast and the distant Loire region are the lush fields,
dairy farms and orchards of the Pays d'Auge around Lisieux and
the rich meadows of the Perche region, famous for its horses. To
the the west, the rocky gorges and wooded hills of the Suisse
Normande, such as the Roche d'Oëtre, are perfect for hiking,
walking and canoeing.

As well as the traditional timber-framed buildings, there are
churches and houses of mellow, creamy limestone; this same
material was once shipped from the busy port of Caen to build
new cathedrals in the Norman-ruled kingdom of England.

Caen

Traffic roars around Caen's floodlit medieval château, which, along with the Église St-Pierre opposite its town gate, provides the main focus of this busy port on the River Orne. Three-quarters of the city was destroyed after the massive bombardments of World War II, but the modern, businesslike centre still retains a few of its old buildings in golden Caen limestone. On the outskirts, the cost and legacy of war are considered in the remarkable Mémorial (➤ 48–49).

✚ 6E

Abbaye aux Dames

Duke William, later the Conqueror, defied a papal ruling to marry his distant cousin, Matilda of Flanders, and both were excommunicated in 1051. Eight years later, Abbot Lanfranc of Bec persuaded the Pope to lift the exclusion in return for the founding of two abbeys: the Abbaye aux Dames, northeast of the centre, where Matilda would be interred, and the Abbaye aux Hommes (➤ opposite), William's mausoleum. Matilda's simple black-marble tomb lies in the chancel of the abbey church, La Trinité.

✚ *Caen 4b* ✉ Place de la Reine Mathilde ☎ 02 31 06 98 98 ⊗ Guided tours: daily 2:30, 4. Closed 1 Jan, 1 May, 25 Dec ✋ Free

Abbaye aux Hommes

Viewed from the east across a geometric formal garden, the abbey buildings and Église St-Étienne present a striking mixture of styles. To the left are the classical 18th-century monastic buildings, now housing the town hall; to the right the chancel of the abbey church, busy with early Gothic spires, turrets and buttresses. The original west façade is simpler, its elegant 11th-century towers crowned in the 13th century with octagonal spires. The Conqueror's fragmentary remains – one thigh bone – lie under an inscribed stone by the altar; the rest were stolen when Huguenots raided the church in the 16th century.

http://abbaye-aux-hommes.cef.fr

✠ *Caen 1c* ✉ Esplanade Jean-Marie Louvel ☎ 02 31 30 42 81
🕓 Mon–Thu 8–6, Fri 8–5, Sat, Sun and public hols 9:15–1, 2–5:45. Guided tours: daily 9:30, 11, 2:30, 4. Closed 1 Jan, 1 May, 25 Dec ✋ Inexpensive

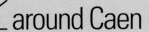

around Caen

a walk

This walk takes you from Mathilde's resting-place, Abbaye aux Dames, to that of William the Conqueror, visiting the main monuments and streets between the mausoleum churches.

Leaving the abbey church of La Trinité (place de la Reine Mathilde, ➤ 126), turn left and go down rue Manissier. At the end turn right on to rue Basse and continue to the pedestrian crossing; then turn left (rue Samuel Bochard) to reach place Courtonne.

Hotels and restaurants line this large open square that takes in the yachting marina and port at one end, and the lone Tour Guillaume-le-Roy at the other.

Turn right along rue des Prairies St-Gilles to rejoin rue Basse, then right up rue Buquet. Cross into rue du Vaugueux.

Some of Caen's most atmospheric restaurants can be found in this secluded cobbled area, one of the few surviving old streets.

At the end of the street cross the road to the castle: enter the grounds over the long drawbridge. Exit from the Musée des Beaux-Arts to Église St-Pierre (➤ 130), and cross into rue St-Pierre.

The Musée de la Poste, on this bustling shopping street, occupies the best example of timber-framed architecture in the city centre .

Just beyond the Église St-Sauveur (also known as Notre-Dame de Froide-rue), turn right into rue Froide. Continue to rue St-Sauveur and (left) place St-Sauveur.

Elegant town houses lead from Vieux St-Sauveur, a medieval church gradually being restored after extensive wartime damage, to the Palais de Justice whose classical columns dominate place Fontette.

Cross the square to the formal gardens for a magnificent view of Duke William's Abbaye aux Hommes (➤ 127).

Distance About 5km (3 miles)
Time 1.5 hours, without visits
Start point Abbaye aux Dames ✚ Caen 4b
End point Abbaye aux Hommes ✚ Caen 1c
Lunch Alcide (€€) ✉ 1 place Courtonne, Caen ☎ 02 31 44 18 06

Château

Another of Duke William's foundations, the château was strengthened and embellished over several centuries. Its massive donjon was destroyed during the Revolution, and more damage followed during World War II, but the restored walls are still impressive, situated on a rocky eminence surrounded by a grassed-over moat. Within the walls are the **Musée des Beaux-Arts** with its fine collection of Flemish, French and Italian paintings from the 16th to the 20th century, and the **Musée de Normandie** (in the former governor's residence), which traces the region's history.

🕂 *Caen 3b* ✉ Rue Montoir-Poissonnerie, entry through Porte sur la Ville 👆 Free

Musée des Beaux-Arts

✉ Château precinct ☎ 02 31 30 47 70 🕐 Wed–Mon 9:30–6. Closed 1 Jan, Easter, 1 May, Ascension, 11 Nov, 25 Dec 👆 Free; temporary exhibitions inexpensive

Musée de Normandie

✉ Château precinct ☎ 02 31 30 47 60; www.musee-de-normandie.caen.fr 🕐 Wed–Mon 9:30–6 👆 Free; temporary exhibitions inexpensive

Église St-Pierre

St-Pierre's 72m (236ft) spire provides a useful landmark within the town's confusing road system. There has been a church on the site since the 7th century, but the present building is mainly 13th- to 16th-century. There are some fine carvings inside, particularly on the columns on the northern side of the nave; medieval scenes here include a phoenix rising from the ashes, a unicorn being comforted by a young woman, and the trials of the Knights of the Round Table.

🕂 *Caen 3c* ✉ Rue Montoir-Poissonnerie 🍴 Choice of restaurants, cafés and bars (€–€€€)

More to see in Calvados and Orne

ALENÇON

Alençon is a pleasant, unspoiled town of narrow streets and squares, whose centre is dominated by the neo-classical Palais de Justice and the grim château gatehouse. The nearby market hall is a striking circular, glass-domed building. The town made a name for itself when Louis XIV's minister Colbert established a lace industry here. Samples of Alençon lace are shown in the Musée des Beaux-Arts et de la Dentelle, housed in a former Jesuit college in the Cour Carrée de la Dentelles.

www.ville-alencon.fr

✚ 19K ▮▮ Choice of restaurants (€€) 🚌 From Argentan 🚆 From Rouen, Cherbourg

ARGENTAN

Argentan provides a good touring centre for excursions into the wooded Suisse Normande. The town itself, which once rivalled Alençon's lace industry, has an impressive Flamboyant church – St-Germain – that stands opposite the turreted 14th-century château (now housing law courts); standing apart from the château is its former chapel, now the tourist information centre. The town was the scene of historic talks in the late 12th century, with papal legates trying to reconcile King Henry II of England and Thomas à Becket; when they failed, Henry's knights set off from Argentan to rid him of his 'turbulent priest'.

www.argentan.fr

✚ 18J ▮▮ Restaurants in town (€–€€) 🚌 From Alençon 🚆 From Rouen, Granville (Paris Montparnasse–Granville line)

ARROMANCHES-LES-BAINS

Fragments of the artificial harbour 'Mulberry B' form a vast semicircle in the sea beyond this quiet seaside resort, a reminder of the D-Day landings of June 1944. Chunks of the harbour also lie on the sandy beach, giving an idea of the sheer size and scale of the operation, an account of which is given in the **Musée du Débarquement.** Visit the excellent clifftop 360-degree cinema that re-creates the landings.

www.arromanches.com

➕ 5D 🍴 Choice of cafés and brasseries (€–€€) 🚌 From Bayeux

Musée du Débarquement

✉ Place du 6 Juin ☎ 02 31 22 34 31 🕐 May–Aug daily 9–7; Sep daily 9–6; Oct, Mar daily 9:30–12:30, 1:30–5:30; Nov, Dec, Feb daily 10–12:30, 1:30–5; Apr daily 9–12:30, 1:30–6. Closed 24, 25, 31 Dec ✋ Moderate

BAYEUX

Bayeux's chief attraction is its tapestry (➤ 40–41), yet the town itself has great charm. An air of quiet prosperity hangs over its old stone and timber-framed buildings; the Aure river flows past

watermills, and the cathedral forms a graceful focus. Built by Odo – sponsor of the tapestry – the cathedral still has its original towers and crypt. The nave's 12th-century arcades are decorated with Romanesque and oriental designs, and interesting frescoes include a portrayal of Thomas à Becket's murder, while angels play musical instruments in the crypt. Beside the cathedral, the Musée Baron Gérard includes porcelain, furniture and paintings. The **Musée Mémorial de la Bataille de Normandie** presents a vivid picture of the Battle of Normandy.
www.bayeux-tourism.com

🔒 5D 🍴 Choice of restaurants (€–€€€) 🚌 From Caen 🚆 From Cherbourg, Caen

Musée Mémorial de la Bataille de Normandie

✉ Boulevard Fabian Ware ☎ 02 31 51 46 90 🕐 Mid-May to mid-Sep daily 9:30–6:30; mid-Sep to Dec daily 10–12:30, 2–6 ✋ Moderate

BEUVRON-EN-AUGE

Set in the heart of the Pays d'Auge, surrounded by orchards, stud farms and grazing cattle, Beuvron-en-Auge must be one of Normandy's prettiest villages. Timber-framed town houses surround the central square, where the steep-roofed *halles* (covered market) contain the Pavé d'Auge restaurant (➤ 59). At the edge of the village the Vieux Manoir, with its cross-braced timbers, is decorated with woodcarvings of faces and figures.

🔒 7E 🍴 Auberge de la Boule d'Or (€–€€), Pavé d'Auge (€€–€€€)

CABOURG

This prosperous seaside resort has retained its 19th-century air of elegance. Dominating the long but featureless promenade is the Grand Hôtel, which lives up to its name and still trades on its association with Marcel Proust; the writer stayed here and based his fictional 'Balbec' on the town. The beach is long and sandy, overlooked by the Grand's wide windows, which recall Proust's descriptions of passers-by gazing at the rich diners in their 'aquarium'.

🚩 6E 🍴 Choice of restaurants and bars (€–€€€) 🚌 From Caen 🚆 From Lisieux in season

CANAPVILLE

The bishops of Lisieux once resided here in the attractive timber-framed manor house set between the Touques river and the busy N177. Built between the 13th and 15th centuries, the **Manoir des Évêques** is set in attractive gardens and has interesting carvings – including one of a bishop's head on the gatepost. Inside there is 18th-century furniture, Chinese porcelain and oriental sculpture on display.

🚏 7D 🍴 Restaurants in village (€–€€) 🚌 From Lisieux

Manoir des Évêques

☎ 02 31 65 24 75; www.manoirdeseveques.fr 🕐 Jul, Aug Wed–Mon 2–7 💰 Moderate

CHÂTEAU DE BALLEROY

A long tree-lined road leads through Balleroy to this early 17th-century mansion overlooking the Drôme Valley. The symmetrical pink and grey château, built by François Mansart for Jean de Choisy, was bought in 1970 by the American publishing magnate Malcolm Forbes. His passion for ballooning inspired the Musée des Ballons, which traces the sport's history from the first passenger flight in 1783 to barrage balloons of World War II.

www.chateau-balleroy.com

🚏 4E ✉ 15km (9 miles) southwest of Bayeux, off D572 ☎ 02 31 21 60 61 🕐 Mid-Mar to mid-Oct Wed–Mon 10–6; Jul–Aug daily 10–6; rest of year Mon, Wed–Fri 10–12, 1:30–5 💰 Moderate 🚌 From Bayeux

CHÂTEAU DE CARROUGES

An ornate stone gatehouse with four steep-roofed towers provides the entrance to this handsome red-brick building set in attractive

parkland beyond the village of Carrouges. Until the 1930s the château was owned by the Le Veneur de Tillières family, who had lived there for nearly 500 years. The earliest part of the present building was built in the 14th century for Jean de Carrouges. Tours lead upstairs and downstairs: from the panelled Louis XI room, where the king himself stayed, to the 15th-century kitchen arrayed with pots and pans. A craft centre and the Parc Naturel Régional Normandie-Maine information centre are based in the park.

✚ 18K ☎ 02 33 27 20 32

🕐 Apr to mid-Jun, Sep 10–12, 2–6; mid-Jun to Aug, 9:30–12, 2–6:30; Oct–Mar 10–12, 2–4:30. Closed 1 Jan, 1 May, 1 and 11 Nov, 25 Dec

♿ Moderate 🍴 La Boulangerie: teas and breakfasts for groups (€€)

🚌 From Argentan/Alençon

CHÂTEAU DE FONTAINE-HENRY

As the D141 follows the Mue river towards Fontaine-Henry, the château can be glimpsed among the trees across the valley; but only when the road has climbed through the quiet Caen-stone hamlet is the building's extraordinary façade revealed. The earliest part, built in the 1490s for the Harcourt family, is a stone wing decorated with elegant carvings. The later wing, added in about 1550, is completely different: top-heavy with precipitous slate roofs that rise as high as the main walls below. Still privately owned, the château houses a collection of 17th- to 18th-century French paintings, as well as porcelain, furniture and 16th-century costumes. There is a late medieval chapel in the grounds.

www.chateau-de-fontaine-henry.com

➕ 5E ☎ 06 89 84 85 57 🕒 Easter to mid-Jun, mid-Sep to Oct Sat, Sun, public hols, 2:30–6:30; Wed–Mon, mid-Jun to mid-Sep 2:30–6:30

✋ Moderate 🍴 Restaurant at Basly, northeast, and in village (€€)

🚌 From Caen

CHÂTEAU D'O

Best places to see, pages 42–43.

CHÂTEAU DE SASSY

Beyond the hamlet of St-Christophe-le-Jajolet, on the brow of a wooded hill, this 18th-century red-brick château overlooks its terraced garden. It was begun in 1760 and passed in 1850 to the dukes of Audriffet-Pasquier, the current owners. Items on display include tapestries and a lock of hair cut from Louis XVI's head; the doomed king presented it to a member of the Pasquier family, who had acted as his defence counsel.

➕ 18J ☎ 02 33 35 32 66 🕒 Easter–Oct daily 3–6; grounds all year daily

✋ Moderate 🚌 From Alençon to St-Christophe-le-Jajolet

CHÂTEAU DE VENDEUVRE

Set among formal flower beds and an ornamental water garden, this 18th-century château houses some intriguing curiosities, including a chair designed for fashion-conscious women in panniers (the 'saddlebags' worn to widen skirts). The main attraction, though, is the Musée de Mobilier Miniature, a collection of tiny masterpieces made from the 16th century to the present day. These include silverware, embroidery, furniture and cutlery, all in immaculate, scaled-down detail; one of the most popular items is a miniature bed, complete with hangings, made in the 18th century for the pet cat of Louis XV's daughter.

www.vendeuvre.com

➕ 18H ☎ 02 31 40 93 83 ⏱ May–Sep daily 11–6; Apr, Oct daily 2–6
✋ Moderate

CLÉCY

Houseboats, restaurants and bars line the Orne river on the approach to Clécy, which is centred on its 19th-century church.

The main attraction of the village is its position in the Suisse Normande, surrounded by hill walks and viewpoints, one of the most popular being the Pain de Sucre, which looks out across the Orne Valley. Model trains run around a miniature landscape of the Suisse Normande at the Musée du Chemin de Fer Miniature (➤ 69).

🔱 17H 🍴 Cafés and restaurants in town and on riverside (€–€€€)

CRÈVECŒUR-EN-AUGE

An attractive cluster of traditional timber-framed and stone buildings represents the Château de Crèvecœur, founded here in the 11th century. Within the moated complex are the remains of the donjon and its enclosure, and the chapel and workshops which were eventually taken over as farm buildings. These have been restored by the present owners, the Schlumberger Foundation, whose work in the oil industry is covered in an exhibition next door to the site.

www.chateau-de-crevecoeur.com

🔱 7E ☎ 02 31 63 02 45 🕐 Apr–Sep, daily 11–6 (Jul–Aug 11–7); Oct Sun only 2–6. Closed Tue in Apr, May, Jun, Sep 🖐 Inexpensive 🍴 Auberge du Cheval Blanc (€€) 🚌 From Lisieux during school terms

DEAUVILLE

Two Côte Fleurie resorts, Deauville and Trouville, face each other across the Touques river – but it is Deauville that attracts the moneyed tourist. Eugène Cornuché built the racecourse, casino and les Planches, a long seafront boardwalk, in 1910, and each summer the big spenders continue to arrive; beach huts boast the names of celebrities past and present. From July to the end of August events include the American Film Festival, the Grand Prix horse race and a tennis tournament; out of season the town hibernates.

www.deauville.org

➕ 7D 🍴 Choice of restaurants and bars (€€–€€€) 🚌 From Caen and le Havre 🚉 From Lisieux in summer

DIVES-SUR-MER

Duke William embarked from this former inland port to conquer England in 1066, and later had a church built here, Notre-Dame, much restored and rebuilt since. Near by are the town's wooden *halles* (covered markets), built in the 15th century so that the local monastery could collect market duties from the traders. Craft shops and a restaurant have been set up near the yachting marina in a 16th-century inn, now known as the Village Guillaume-le-Conquérant.

www.dives-sur-mer.com

➕ 7E 🍽 Restaurants (€–€€) 🚌 From Caen 🚃 From Lisieux in season

DOMFRONT

Old and new Domfront sprawl from the ruined hilltop fortress high above the Varenne river. In the upper quarter, stone and timber-framed houses seem to grow from the ramparts and towers, and huddle for safety over narrow cobbled streets. The fortress was built in 1092 by the son of William the Conqueror, later King Henry I of England. On the riverside at the bottom of the hill is the 11th- to 12th-century Église Notre-Dame-sur-l'Eau, where Thomas à Becket is said to have celebrated mass in 1166. The summer medieval festival (dates

vary) features street theatre, music, markets and banquets, all in period costume.

www.domfront.com

➕ 16K 🍽 Restaurants in new town (€€) 🚌 From Argentan, or from Caen to Flers, then local bus from Flers

FALAISE

William the Conqueror's birthplace has become the subject of fierce controversy. It was at Falaise that his father, Robert, took a fancy to Arlette, a tanner's daughter, as she washed her clothes in the river; rejecting all secrecy, she later met Robert inside the **château** and subsequently gave birth to William there. The modern controversy concerns the restoration of the site's 12th-century donjon, its chapel, and the 13th-century Tour de Talbot. Bruno Decaris's concrete and steel additions have shocked traditionalists, but their sudden plunging views and glimpses of thick stonework give a sense of the former military might often missing at similar monuments. A glass floor reveals the foundations of Duke Robert's stronghold, and delicately carved windows can be seen behind etched reinforced glass. A walk around the top of the Tour de Talbot offers dizzy views over the Ante Valley.

In the town, the **Musée André Lemaître** displays work by the local artist who painted landscapes inspired by the area. The Musée Août 44 traces the fighting that took place here in World War II, and at the Automates Avenue there's an absorbing collection of clockwork tableaux dating from the 1920s.

www.otsifalaise.com

➕ 18H 🍴 La Fine Fourchette, rue G Clemenceau (€–€€) 🚌 From Caen

Château

☎ 02 31 41 61 44; www.chateau-guillaume-leconquerant.fr ✪ Mid-Feb to Jun, Sep–Dec daily

10–6; Jul, Aug daily 10–7 🖐 Inexpensive ❓ Guided tours every hour; English tour 1:30

Musée André Lemaître

✉ Boulevard de la Libération ☎ 02 31 90 02 43 🕐 Daily 10–12:30, 1:30–6. Closed mid-Jan to mid-Feb 🖐 Inexpensive

LE HARAS DU PIN

Louis XIV's minister Colbert set up the national stud in 1665, but it was abolished briefly during the Revolution. Re-established in the 19th century, its breeds include Percherons, Norman cobs and English thoroughbreds. Beyond the wrought-iron gate, topped with a gold horse's head, staff live and work in the 18th-century château, with the stable wings on either side. Walks and rides lead off into woodland, and the gentle Pays d'Auge landscape stretches into the distance.

✚ 19J ☎ 02 33 36 68 68 🕐 Guided tour: Apr to mid-Oct daily 9:30–6; mid-Oct to Mar daily 2–5 🖐 Moderate 🍴 Restaurant near by (€€) 🚌 From Argentan to Nonant-le-Pin

HONFLEUR

Best places to see, pages 46–47.

LISIEUX

Pilgrims come in thousands to Lisieux, the town where Sainte Thérèse lived as a child. It is also the main centre of the Pays d'Auge. Apart from a scatter of old houses near the 13th-century cathedral and the Hôtel de Ville, the centre is largely modern and nondescript; the main interest lies in the places associated with Thérèse, including **les Buissonnets** where she lived as a girl. The massive, domed Basilique Ste-Thérèse, consecrated in the 1950s, stands out among concrete and glass office blocks; its 45m (147ft) belfry houses no fewer than 44 bells, and an exhibition describes the life led by Thérèse and other Carmelite nuns. The saint's relics are kept in the Chapelle du Carmel, guarded by a statue of the Virgin that was once owned by her family.
www.lisieux-tourisme.com

➕ 7E 🍴 Choice of restaurants (€–€€€)
🚌 From Rouen 🚆 From Rouen, Évreux
(Paris–Dives line)
Les Buissonnets
✉ 22 Chemin des Buissonnets ☎ 02 31
48 55 08 🕐 Mid-Mar to Sep daily 9–12,
2–6; Oct, Feb, Mar daily 10–12, 2–5;
Nov–Jan daily 10–12, 2–4 ✋ Free

MORTAGNE-AU-PERCHE

Former capital of the Perche, Mortagne stands on a hill overlooking a gentle landscape of meadows, red-roofed farms and wooded hills. Dilapidated houses with wrought-iron balconies line the streets, and the only remaining fortification, the Porte St-Denis, houses a regional museum, the Musée Percheron. The 15th-century Église Notre-Dame has good woodwork around the altar.

Mortagne is best known today for the production of *boudin*, a black sausage celebrated every March in the Festival du Boudin Noir.
www.cdc-mortagne-au-perche.com
➕ 20K 🍴 Choice of restaurants (€–€€) 🚌 From Alençon

ORBEC

This unassuming market town has a good collection of crooked timber-framed houses, including the 16th-century Vieux Manoir that houses the **Musée Municipal,** whose collection of paintings, ceramics and other artefacts recall the history and traditions of the Pays d'Auge. The Église Notre-Dame has a massive belfry, originally a defensive tower in the 15th century but given a more decorative finish in the following century.
www.mairie-orbec.fr
➕ 20H 🍴 Restaurants in town (€–€€€) 🚌 From Lisieux
Musée Municipal
✉ Grande Rue ☎ 02 31 32 58 89 🕐 Jul, Aug Wed–Sun 10–12:30, 3–6;
Easter–All Saints Day, Wed–Sun 10–12, 3–6 ✋ Inexpensive

OUISTREHAM

The ferry port of Ouistreham also offers a cheerful yacht marina and the beach resort of Riva-Bella. Set back from the coast, among suburban villas, are reminders of D-Day's Sword Beach: the **Musée du Mur de l'Atlantique,** housed in the German range-finding station, Big Bunker; and the Musée du Débarquement No 4 Commando, opposite the casino, with military exhibits from World War II.

www.ville-ouistreham.fr

✚ 6E 🍴 Choice of cafés and restaurants near ferry terminal and beach (€–€€€) 🚌 From Caen

Musée du Mur de l'Atlantique

✉ Avenue du 6 Juin ☎ 02 31 97 28 69 🕐 Feb to mid-Nov daily 10–6 (till 7 Apr–Sep) ✋ Moderate

POINTE DU HOC

Nothing evokes the scale and violence of the 1944 landings more poignantly than this 30m (100ft) clifftop position overlooking Omaha Beach. This German observation point was heavily bombarded, thus allowing American Rangers to climb the sheer rocks, albeit with heavy casualties; their story is told in the Musée des Rangers at Grandcamp-Maisy, 5km (3 miles) west. A viewing platform and memorial have been set up on the headland, a surreal landscape of modern megaliths: massive slabs of concrete lie scattered amid vast craters, now softened by grass. From the platform there are clear views of the invasion coast and the site itself, now silent except for the call of seagulls.

✚ 4D 🍴 Choice of restaurants at Grandcamp-Maisy (€–€€€) 🚌 From Bayeux to Grandcamp-Maisy

PONT-L'ÉVÊQUE

Cheese is the principal claim to fame of this historic town in the Touques Valley. Its soft and creamy speciality was first produced in the 12th century, when the town was known as Angelot; it only took the name of Pont-l'Évêque some 500 years later. Attractive timber-framed buildings survive, as well as the Flamboyant Église St-Michel, where plaques commemorate the victims of the Franco-Prussian War and other conflicts. The **Musée du Calvados et des Métiers Anciens** describes traditional methods used in making calvados.

In the nearby Château de Betteville, south of town, the Musée de la Belle Époque de l'Automobile has a collection of vintage vehicles (1800–1960s).

www.pontleveque.com

✚ 7E 🍴 Choice of restaurants (€–€€€) 🚌 From Lisieux

Musée du Calvados et des Métiers Anciens

✉ Distillerie du Père Magloire, route de Trouville ☎ 02 31 64 30 31
🕐 Guided tours Apr, Oct 11, 2:30, 3:30, 4:30; May–Sep 10:30, 11:30, 2:30, 3:30, 4:30, 5:30 ✋ Inexpensive

along the D-Day beaches

This drive passes through many of the sites associated with the D-Day landings.

From Caen take the D514 northeast towards Ouistreham.

A short detour (follow signs) leads to Pegasus Bridge, captured by British parachutists on 5 June 1944. Sound-and-light shows take place between April and October.

From Ouistreham (▶ 148) and Sword Beach, continue through St-Aubin and Courseulles (Juno Beach) to Arromanches (▶ 133).

Between Courseulles (with its colourful art-deco casino) and Arromanches, the flat marshes of the Gold Beach area offer wide sea views.

Follow the D514 from Arromanches and turn left on to the D127, joining the D87 before Ryes.

Continue through the village on the D87 to visit the British and Commonwealth cemetery.

From the cemetery return to the D112 and turn left, following the signs to

Sommervieu. Join the D12 into Bayeux (➤ 134). The D6 goes north to Port-en-Bessin and the Musée des Épaves sous-marines du Débarquement (Museum of Underwater Wrecks of the [D-Day] Landings). Follow the D514 along Omaha Beach.

At Colleville-sur-Mer, follow signs for the American cemetery, one of two war cemeteries for US troops.

Return to the D514 and continue west to Pointe du Hoc (➤ 149). Return to the D514 and turn right, continuing to Grandcamp-Maisy and the Musée des Rangers. The D199 goes south and joins the D113 (left) and D613 (left) for la Cambe and the German cemetery.

To continue to Utah Beach, take the N13 west, then the D913 to Ste-Marie-du-Mont, then drive to the coast.

Distance 80km (50 miles) to la Cambe; a further 28km (17 miles) to Utah Beach
Time 3.5 hours to la Cambe without stops
Start point Caen ✚ 6E
End point La Cambe ✚ 4D
Lunch Le Lion d'Or (€€) B71 rue St-Jean, Bayeux ☎ 02 31 22 15 64

ROCHE D'OËTRE

A track leads from the roadside to this 118m (73ft) rocky precipice that offers some of the best views of the Suisse Normande's wooded slopes. A viewing table points out the main landmarks (take care – there's nothing between you and the drop): the panorama extends over the Orne Valley and the Rouvre gorges, and southeast towards the Lac du Rabodanges. An information centre has maps, leaflets, a shop and restaurant (closed in winter), plus a small museum about the area.

The small town of Pont-d'Ouilly, downriver, is a good centre for exploring the area, and has pleasant walks alongside the fast-flowing Orne.

🚩 17J 🍴 Restaurant at information centre (€–€€) 🚌 From Caen to Clécy

ST-GERMAIN-DE-LIVET

Hidden in the dip of an isolated tributary of the Touques is a château straight from a children's picture book. The two surviving wings join at the ornate gatehouse: a 15th-century timber-framed range and a turreted 16th-century wing, its ostentatious chequered walls built using limestone, and green-glazed and red bricks. Frescos are preserved in the older house, while the later wing has a gallery of 19th-century paintings and a room decorated with terracotta tiles. The decorative style of brickwork found on the chateau can be seen also in the transept of the church opposite.

🚩 7E ☎ 02 31 31 00 03 🕐 Feb–Nov, 11–6. Closed Dec, Jan and first 2 weeks in Nov 🖐 Moderate 🍴 Restaurants at Lisieux (€–€€€) 🚌 From Lisieux

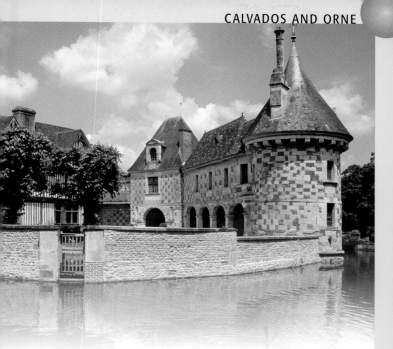

ST-PIERRE-SUR-DIVES

On Monday mornings this small country town bursts into life as the market sets up in the cavernous, barn-like **halles.** Inside, the beamed roof echoes with the cacophony of ducks, turkeys, chickens and stall-holders, and the gabble continues at the brick stalls outside. Originally built in the 11th century, the hall was faithfully rebuilt after World War II using 290,000 wooden dowels and not a single nail. In the town's large church, once part of a Benedictine abbey, the 'Meridian', a line carved across the nave, flanked by signs of the zodiac and almost worn away in parts, indicates the position of the sun at noon.

www.mairie-saint-pierre-sur-dives.fr

✚ 18H 🍴 Restaurants, cafés (€–€€) 🚌 From Lisieux (during school terms)
Les Halles

🕐 Apr–Oct 8–8; otherwise apply to tourist office ❓ Antiques market first Sun of every month ☎ 02 31 23 29 21

SÉES

Sées, close to the source of the Orne, on whose banks the town stands, has been an important religious centre since AD 400, when Saint Latuin became its first bishop. The town is dominated by its splendid Gothic cathedral, the classical bishop's palace, and the former canons' lodgings that now house the **Musée Départemental d'Art Religieux,** with its collection of sculpture, paintings and decorative objects. The western façade of the cathedral was bolstered with buttresses in the 16th century when it began to lean dangerously. Dramatic 13th-century stained-glass windows light the transept, and delicate tracery decorates the nave arcades and windows. In the porch, faded carvings can still be made out, including a cat carrying its kitten, and a double-headed eagle.

✚ 19K 🍴 Choice of restaurants and cafés (€–€€€) 🚌 From Alençon
🚊 From Rouen

Musée Départemental d'Art Religieux

✉ 7 place du Général-de-Gaulle ☎ 02 33 81 23 00 🕐 Jul–Sep Wed–Mon 10–6 💰 Inexpensive

THURY-HARCOURT

This pleasant Suisse Normande centre, beside the Orne river, acquired its name from two sources: 'Thury', according to local legend, from a Viking cry, *Thor Aïe*; and Harcourt from the eponymous family who lived in the 11th-century château. Much of the former fortress was destroyed during World War II and only the skeletal façade remains, surrounded by restored gardens and a park.

✚ 17H 🍴 Choice of restaurants near river (€€–€€€) 🚌 From Caen

TROUVILLE

Deauville's neighbour across the Touques estuary, Trouville is the more appealing and cheerful of the two resorts, with its fishing boats, the tree-lined boulevard Fernand Moureaux, and a wide sandy beach and boardwalk. Garish lights advertise the Louisiana Follies at the salmon-pink casino, and fish, reptiles and insects are on display at the Aquarium écologique. Set back from the seafront, the Église Notre-Dame de Bon-Secours has intricate stained-glass windows and an ornate 19th-century façade, and the **Musée Villa Montebello** houses paintings by Eugène Boudin; the museum also traces the history of sea bathing, which became the rage here in the 1820s.

www.trouvillesurmer.org

⊞ 7D 🍴 Choice of restaurants along boulevard Fernand Moureaux and rue Carnot (€–€€) 🚌 From Lisieux and Caen 🚉 From Lisieux

Musée Villa Montebello

✉ 64 rue du Gal Leclerc ☎ 02 31 88 16 26 🕐 25 Mar–28 May, 24 Jun–24 Sep Wed–Mon 2–5:30 💵 Inexpensive; free Wed

VIRE

This major route junction in a
bend of the Vire river is visited by
an endless stream of traffic. At place 6 Juin 1944 cars besiege the
13th-century gate and belfry, the **Porte-Horloge.** There are few
other survivors of the historic town that was devastated in World
War II: among shops south of the gateway are two defensive
towers, and on an eminence above the river are remains of a 12th-
century donjon. Local traditions are recalled in the Musée de Vire,
set in the quiet cobbled courtyard of the Hôtel-Dieu.

Textile mills once dotted the surrounding *bocage*. Here during
the 15th century, in the district known as Vaux de Vire, Olivier
Basselin penned his popular poems and songs, the precursors
of vaudeville.

www.vire-tourisme.com

 16H 🍴 Choice of restaurants and cafés (€–€€€) 🚌 From Caen 🚃 From
Granville/Argentan (Paris Montparnasse line)

Porte-Horloge

✉ Place du 6 Juin 1944 ☎ 02 31 66 28 50 (tourist office) 🕐 Jul to mid-Sep
Mon–Sat 2:30–6:30 💷 Inexpensive

HOTELS

ALENÇON

Hôtel Le Grand St-Michel (€–€€)
Good-value, traditional service in a quiet Logis de France hotel.
✉ 7 rue du Temple ☎ 02 33 26 04 77 🕑 Closed Jul

BAYEUX

Churchill Hotel (€€–€€€)
In the heart of town, a quiet and welcoming retreat with free parking and individually styled rooms.
✉ 14 rue St-Jean ☎ 02 31 21 31 80 🕑 Closed Jan

Hôtel du Lion d'Or (€€–€€€)
See page 75.

CABOURG

Grand Hôtel (€€€)
See page 74.

Hôtel de Paris (€€)
Central hotel in a timber-framed building, with a wide range of room prices. Parking.
✉ 39 avenue de la Mer ☎ 02 31 91 31 34

CAEN

Au Saint-Jean (€–€€)
Good-value rooms with no frills but all basic facilities; helpful staff and its own garage. Near the Église St-Jean, south of the château.
✉ 20 rue des Martyrs ☎ 02 31 86 23 35

Best Western le Dauphin (€€–€€€)
See page 74.

Hôtel des Cordeliers (€)
Wide range of rooms with a choice of prices – choose what best suits your budget. Set in its own garden.
✉ 4 rue des Cordeliers ☎ 02 31 86 37 15

Hôtel Saint-Étienne (€)

A good budget choice with character, set in an 18th-century stone building within reach of the Abbaye aux Hommes. Some rooms without showers, but all have baths.

✉ 2 rue de l'Académie ☎ 02 31 86 35 82

Hôtel de l'Univers (€–€€)

Small and basic motel near the quayside, with rather drearily decorated but clean rooms, some sharing toilet facilities. Set on a large and busy square with plenty of public parking.

✉ 12 quai Vendeuvre, place Courtonne ☎ 02 31 85 46 14

HONFLEUR
L'Absinthe (€€€)

See page 74.

Hotel Cheval Blanc (€€€)

Rather special hotel in a historic 15th-century building overlooking the fishing port. Comfortable rooms and babysitting service available. Some rooms have hydro-massage or a jacuzzi.

✉ 2 quai des Passagers ☎ 02 31 81 65 00 🕙 Closed Jan

ORBEC
Côté Jardin (€–€€)

See page 74.

SÉES
Hôtel Le Dauphin (€€)

Logis de France hotel near the old market hall, with good breakfasts and generous evening meals.

✉ 31 place des Halles ☎ 02 33 27 80 07 🕙 Closed Jan

TROUVILLE
Hôtel les Sablettes (€–€€)

Quiet hotel with a garden near the town centre. Slightly old-fashioned in style but good value.

✉ 15 rue Paul Besson ☎ 02 31 88 10 66

RESTAURANTS

ALENÇON

Au Petit Vatel (€–€€)

The good, hearty, traditional food here includes excellent puddings and an interesting selection of fish dishes.

✉ 72 place Cdt Desmeulles ☎ 02 33 26 23 78 ◉ Lunch, dinner. Closed first 3 weeks Aug, Sun eve, Wed

La Renaissance (€–€€)

Cool bar for hanging out with Alençon's in-crowd and grabbing a bite before painting the town rouge. Open till past midnight, except for Sundays when doors close at 8pm.

✉ 4 rue Saint Blaise ☎ 02 33 26 01 10 ◉ Lunch, dinner

ARROMANCHES-LES-BAINS

La Marine (€€–€€€)

A small hotel-restaurant overlooking the port, with good seafood. Friendly service and high standards of cuisine.

✉ 2 quai Canada ☎ 02 31 22 34 19 ◉ Lunch, dinner. Closed mid-Nov to mid-Feb

BAYEUX

Le Lion d'Or (€€–€€€)

The traditional menu at this ancient coaching inn is accompanied by a very good range of wines. A long-established and popular choice with tourists.

✉ 71 rue St-Jean ☎ 02 31 92 06 90 ◉ Lunch, dinner. Closed mid-Dec to mid-Jan, Mon lunch, Sat lunch

BEUVRON-EN-AUGE

Le Pavé d'Auge (€€–€€€)

See page 59.

CAEN

Alcide (€–€€)

An affordable and popular option in the town centre. Classic French dishes, bistro-style, are served to a loyal local clientele.

Generous helpings of mussels, crêpes and meat dishes.

✉ 1 place Courtonne ☎ 02 31 44 18 06 🕐 Lunch, dinner. Closed late Dec, Sat

Le Carlotta (€–€€)

True turn-of-the-20th-century brasserie. Blend of traditional dishes, such as steak tartare, with imaginative modern sauces for fresh fish. Huge portions for the larger appetites.

✉ 16 quai Vendeuvre ☎ 02 31 86 68 99 🕐 Lunch, dinner. Closed Sun

Le P'tit B (€€–€€€)

The most highly regarded restaurant in Caen, with prices to match. Regional specialities include Caen *tripes*, chicken in creamy *vallée d'Auge* sauce, Vire chitterlings, pigs' trotters *galette* and other dishes – each guaranteed to have their own added unique touches.

✉ 15–17 rue du Vaugueux ☎ 02 31 93 50 76 🕐 Lunch, dinner

Le Zodiaque (€€)

Twelve signs of the zodiac in the decor, but even more ways with beef, steaks and duck. Astrological theme apart, a good place for hearty local grills.

✉ 15 quai Eugène-Meslin ☎ 02 31 84 46 31 🕐 Lunch, dinner. Closed Mon eve, Tue eve, Sun, hols, Aug

DEAUVILLE
L'Augeval (€€–€€€)

There are many seafront seafood restaurants in the resort, but the best are within the hotels. In summer L'Augeval serves traditional Norman dishes on the terrace facing the pool.

✉ 15 avenue Hocquart de Turtot ☎ 02 31 81 13 18 🕐 Lunch, dinner

DIVES-SUR-MER
Dupont (€€)

A pretty pâtisserie – right next to the church – with a tiny *salon de thé* at the back. Simple meals (pâté, pizza, etc), or take your pick from the delicious offerings in the shop.

✉ Rue Hélène Boucher ☎ 02 31 91 04 30 🕐 Lunch, afternoon tea

HONFLEUR

Le Chat Qui Pêche (€–€€)

Traditional cuisine from around France's ports, blended with good Norman favourites such as duckling and lamb.

✉ 5 place Arthur Boudin ☎ 02 31 89 35 35 🕐 Lunch, dinner

La Cidrerie (€€)

A *crêperie* that prides itself on traditional *galettes* and *crêpes*, washed down with cider, *poiré*, *pommeau* or calvados, or one of its own creations such as P'tio Punch or l'Épiscopal.

✉ 26 place Hamelin ☎ 02 31 89 59 85 🕐 Lunch, dinner. Closed Wed

Le Corsaire (€–€€)

An intimate dining room overlooking the church. Tables are set outside; inside the restaurant is warm and cosy, with an open fire. Squid, chicken in calvados, fish kebabs and guinea fowl braised in calvados are among the offerings.

✉ 22 place Ste-Catherine ☎ 02 31 89 12 80 🕐 Lunch, dinner

Le Vieux Honfleur (€€–€€€)

See page 59.

ORBEC

L'Orbecquoise (€€–€€€)

An initmate restaurant with a log fire, serving stylishly prepared Norman dishes. Reasonable set menus.

✉ 60 rue Grande ☎ 02 31 62 44 99 🕐 Lunch, dinner

TROUVILLE

La Guinguette (€–€€)

Seafood, fish dishes and *tripes à la mode de Caen* served in a friendly, small restaurant with pavement tables, overlooking the river and fishing boats.

✉ 50–52 boulevard Fernand Moureaux ☎ 02 31 88 42 80 🕐 Lunch, dinner

La Marine (€–€€)

See page 59.

La Moulerie (€–€€)

All manner of *moules*, including *moules Normande*, in a riverside restaurant.

✉ 76 boulevard Fernand Moureaux ☎ 02 31 81 59 00 🕐 Lunch, dinner

SHOPPING

FASHION
Anne Fontaine

The designer who all but reinvented the white shirt in *chic couture* is famous for the purity and simplicity of her women's fashions. A cut above the standard *matelot* jerseys in rival windows.

✉ 7 quai Saint-Étienne, Honfleur ☎ 02 31 89 00 53

Port Marine

Lots of caps and stripy tops in this welcoming and friendly seafarers' outfitters.

✉ 22 quai Félix Faure, Port en Bessin, north of Bayeux ☎ 02 31 21 72 83
🕐 Closed Wed (except Jul, Aug)

Troc-Chic

Vintage clothes dating from the 1940s to the 1960s.

✉ 80 rue des Bains, Trouville ☎ 02 31 81 09 19

FOOD
Charlotte Corday

Calvados and apple-flavoured chocolates give the treats at this trendy sweetshop a very Norman twist.

✉ 114 rue Saint-Jean, Caen ☎ 02 31 86 33 25 🕐 Closed Sun, Mon

Aux Fromages de France

The place for cheeses, farmhouse meat dishes and ciders.

✉ 116 rue Saint-Jean, Caen ☎ 02 31 86 14 53

La Petite Chine

Fresh pastries, pains d'épices, calvados and chocolates; a small tea room at the back.

✉ 14–16 rue du Dauphin, Honfleur ☎ 02 31 89 36 52

GIFTS

Agate

Imaginative, and sometimes bizarre, jewellery.

✉ 21 rue des Logettes, Honfleur ☎ 02 31 89 53 88

Artagor

Arts and crafts, including mosaic mirrors, painted lamps, hats and jewellery – unusual souvenirs.

✉ 4 rue Buquet, Caen ☎ 02 31 93 16 00

Le Bois Dormant

Wonderful wooden toys and games for children – tops, trains, drums, jigsaws – in the traditional style. Opposite Église St-Sauveur.

✉ 9 rue Froide, Caen ☎ 02 31 85 35 01

Family Broc

Open every day of the week, this antique shop is the ideal place for art lovers to pick up a quality memento of a region that has inspired generations of painters.

✉ 223 rue de Bayeux, Caen ☎ 02 31 73 00 01

Naphtaline

Inspired by the Bayeux tapestry, buy needlework-themed gifts from cushions to kits, napkins to curtains.

✉ 14–16 parvis de la Cathédrale, Bayeux ☎ 02 31 21 50 03 🕓 Closed Jan, Feb and Sun (out of season)

La Palette

Hematite and crystals, all ready to wear. Jewellery made from minerals and rocks.

✉ 8 rue de Paris, Trouville ☎ 02 31 88 13 75

Le Sémaphore

Ship compasses and bells, lanterns, sailor's caps, porthole mirrors, and other gifts for the seadog who has everything.

✉ 3 rue des Lingots, Honfleur ☎ 02 31 89 97 85

ENTERTAINMENT

LIVE MUSIC VENUES

Café Mancel

Home to the Normandy Jazz Club and popular with lovers of classic swing, jazz and blues sounds.

✉ The Château, Caen ☎ 02 31 86 63 64

La Garsouille

Every Friday at 7:30pm, and on selected weeknights, this is a relaxed live music venue, featuring great jazz and other genres.

✉ 11 rue de Caumont, Caen ☎ 02 31 86 80 27

Hangar Café

The former Book Café is now an informal midweek music venue. Jazz nights once a month.

✉ 9 rue Fresnel, Caen ☎ 02 31 44 09 19 🕐 Tue–Fri

Oxygène B

Music venue for a largely student crowd. Lots of up and coming bands; some themed evenings to attract a non-student audience.

✉ University Campus, Caen ☎ 02 31 56 60 95

THEATRES AND CONCERT HALLS

Théâtre de Caen

Contemporary and traditional productions of music, opera, drama and dance.

✉ 135 boulevard du Maréchal Leclerc, Caen ☎ 02 31 30 48 00

La Théâtre d'Évreux – Scène Nationale

Events include seasons of films in conjunction with the Cinéma Victor Hugo, plus dance, music and drama productions.

✉ Place du Général de Gaulle, Évreux ☎ 02 32 78 85 20

Théâtre de Lisieux

Interesting touring productions, including contemporary drama, at a very traditional venue.

✉ 2 rue au Char, Lisieux ☎ 02 31 61 12 13

La Manche

As you cross the border into Manche and travel towards the head of the Cotentin (Cherbourg) peninsula, the landscape changes and the population dwindles. At the base of the Cotentin are the fields and orchards of the *bocage*, characteristically criss-crossed with dense hedges. Empty beaches and sand dunes line the western coast, and at the tip of the peninsula waves crash against wild, granite cliffs.

Valognes

Cherbourg is the biggest centre, with its constant stream of ferry passengers and its busy port, but the most memorable sight in the northwest – indeed in the whole of Normandy – has to be le Mont-St-Michel (➤ 50–51), perched upon the quicksands in the crook between Normandy and Brittany.

ABBAYE DE HAMBYE

Founded in 1145 by Guillaume Paynel, the
Abbaye de Hambye is now a fragile ruin in the
tranquil valley of the Sienne. The transept tower
survives intact and appears to balance
precariously on delicate arches; flying
buttresses and the nave's high lancet windows
add to the impression that the whole structure
could be blown away on the wind. Outbuildings
house Rouen tapestries, sculptures, frescos,
and paintings of the abbey.

✚ 15H ☎ 02 33 61 76 92 ⊕ Guided tours: Apr–Oct
10–12, 2–6. Closed Tue in winter ✋ Inexpensive
🍴 Auberge de l'Abbaye (€€–€€€), on D51 near by

ABBAYE DE LA LUCERNE

Since 1959 the ruins of this 12th-century abbey
in the isolated Thar Valley have undergone
gradual restoration. The monastic church, used
for concerts in the summer, has a Romanesque
doorway and an elaborate 18th-century organ.
There are also remains of a 19th-century
aqueduct, built for a mill in the grounds, along
with the tithe barn, abbot's house and
dovecote. An arcaded Romanesque lavatorium
– a monastic washstand – survives near the old
refectory. Sunday mass is still held in the
church.

www.abbaye-lucerne.fr

✚ 14H ☎ 02 33 48 83 56 ⊕ Mon–Sat 10–12, 2–6:30
(till 5 Oct–Mar), Sun afternoons. Closed Jan–early Mar,
last 2 weeks Oct, Tue in Feb, Mar, Nov and Dec
✋ Inexpensive 🍴 Auberge le Courtil de la
Lucerne (€€)

AVRANCHES

The hilltop town above the Sée river looks out across the estuary to the church of le Mont-St-Michel, originally founded in the 8th century by Bishop Aubert of Avranches after Saint Michael

had appeared to him in a vision. **Les Manuscrits du Mont-St-Michel** in place d'Estouteville is a collection of illuminated manuscripts associated with the famous abbey, including some fine Romanesque drawings. Behind the town hall, which houses the abbey's library of 14,000 books, are remains of an 11th-century château; steps climb to the donjon and terraced garden, with views inland and over the coast. The 19th-century Église de Notre-Dame-des-Champs is one of three churches built after the old cathedral collapsed in 1790.

www.ville-avranches.fr

✚ 14J 🍴 Choice of restaurants (€–€€) 🚌 From Cherbourg and Granville 🚆 From Caen

Les Manuscrits du Mont-St-Michel

☎ 02 33 79 57 01 🕐 Jul–Aug daily 10–7; May, Jun, Sep Tue–Sun 10–6; Oct–Apr Tue–Sun 10–12:30, 2–5 ✋ Moderate

BARFLEUR

Fishing boats chug in and out, and fishermen mend their nets on the harbourside of this small granite town on the Cotentin's northeast tip. It was near here that William 'Atheling', son of King Henry I, was drowned when the White Ship sank in 1120 – an event that later led to a civil war over the English crown. A narrow passageway runs from the harbour past the 17th-century church to a beach and Normandy's tallest lighthouse (71m/233ft).

www.ville-barfleur.fr

➕ 3C 🍴 Some cafés and bars in town (€–€€) 🚌 From Cherbourg

BARNEVILLE-CARTERET

Barneville-Carteret is a union of two different towns and their beaches. Carteret is the busier resort, with a yachting marina, and a broad sandy beach overlooked by caravans and large faded villas. Ferries travel from the harbour to Jersey and Guernsey.

Barneville, 2km (1.2 miles) away, has an austere 11th-century church with a fortified tower added later. Barneville-Plage, a long, empty stretch of sand, is reached across a cob over the Gerfleur estuary.

www.barneville-carteret.net

➕ 1D 🍴 Restaurants in Barneville and by Carteret beach (€–€€€)

🚌 From Cherbourg

BRICQUEBEC

The impressive ruins of a 14th-century château form the focus of this small market town, whose main street runs right up to the

gatehouse. Inside, the 11-sided donjon is the most prominent of a group of buildings around a pleasant courtyard; one side is taken up with the older Knights' Hall, now the Hostellerie du Château. A walk along the sentry wall leads to the clock tower, which houses a collection of traditional Norman furniture.

www.mairie-briquebec.fr

✚ 2C 🍴 Vieux Château (incorporated into castle); cafés and bars in town (€–€€) 🚌 From Cherbourg

CAP DE LA HAGUE

Heading west from Cherbourg, the road to the northwestern finger of the Cotentin passes the vast, glittering pile of the Usine de Retraitement des Combustibles Nucléaires (nuclear fuel reprocessing centre), then turns left, between high hedges and through the narrow, dark-stone village of Dannery, for the wild rocky headland at Nez de Jobourg. A track leads past an isolated *auberge* to a viewpoint that looks across the coastline and green fields (marred only by the nuclear plant in the distance), and out to sea towards the Channel Islands.

From Dannery the road winds north through a green valley to emerge at the Baie d'Écalgrain, a lovely sweep of coast sheltered by low hills. Beyond the village of Auderville the road comes to an end at Goury, a tiny harbour with a lighthouse and hexagonal lifeboat station; here you can enjoy a meal and watch the waves from the quayside.

www.lahague.org

✚ 1B 🍴 Auberge de Goury, near Goury lifeboat station (€–€€); *crêperie* and Auberge des Grottes in high season at Nez de Jobourg car park (€); restaurants and bars at Auderville (€–€€)

CAROLLES

Carolles is a quiet coastal village with an unassuming beach resort, set between the bustling holiday centre of Granville and Avranches. The location is its main appeal: walks lead from the centre through wooded countryside and along the Vallée du Lude to a remote bay. Carolles-Plage, a stretch of sand backed with beach huts and snack bars, looks north along the spectacular coastline as far as Granville. A viewpoint to the northwest, le Pignon Butor, takes in the Baie du Mont-St-Michel between Granville and the Breton headland of Pointe du Grouin.

✛ 14J 🍴 Snack bars and restaurant at Carolles-Plage (€); bar and *crêperie* in Carolles (€) 🚌 From Granville

CÉRISY-LA-FORÊT

There has been a monastery on the edge of the Cérisy beech woods since the 6th century. St Vigor established a community here about 510, and a later building was commissioned by William the Conqueror's father, Duke Robert. The present Benedictine abbey church dates from the 12th century, built in cream limestone and partly dismantled in 1812. The west end of the nave has gone but the carved choir stalls in the apse have survived. Work continues to strengthen the transept where fissures have appeared. A small museum features statuary, floor tiles and other items rescued from the abbey church, and there is an exhibition of Romanesque art in lower Normandy.

✛ 4E ☎ 02 33 57 34 63 🕓 Daily 9–6:30. Tours Easter–1 Oct daily 10:30–12:30, 2:30–6:30; 2 Oct–1 Nov Sat, Sun and public hols 10:30–12, 2:30–6 ✋ Inexpensive

CHÂTEAU DE GRATOT

Hidden behind a church in quiet farmland are the remains of this château built between the 14th and 18th centuries. The site was later used as farm buildings until renovation by volunteers in the 1960s. A roofless main hall, with a fireplace, is flanked by two towers, one of which – the octagonal Tour à la Fée (Fairy Tower) – is decorated with carved foliage and gargoyles, and topped with a delicate stone trellis. Behind the hall, an arched bridge leads across the moat and steps climb to an empty field, once formal gardens. The château was the home of the Argouges family, and an exhibition in the outbuildings tells their story, including an artist's impression of the gardens in their former glory.

🕇 2E ☎ 02 33 45 18 49 🕓 All year daily 10–7 🖐 Inexpensive
🍴 Le Tourne-Bride (€€), between Gratot and Coutances, on D44

CHÂTEAU DE PIROU

A gatehouse and castellated walkway lead to substantial 12th-century ruins in remote farmland near the dunes of the western Cotentin. The castle was restored several times in subsequent centuries, and in the 15th century was owned by John Falstaff, on whom Shakespeare based his famous character Falstaff. Ramparts protect the various medieval buildings, stacked up on a moated bailey, including the chapel, bakehouse, kitchens and guardroom; a modern tapestry in the knights' hall relates the Norman conquest of southern Italy and Sicily.

www.chateau-pirou.org

🕇 2E ☎ 02 33 46 34 71
🕓 Apr–Sep Wed–Mon
10–12, 2–6:30; Oct–Mar
Wed–Mon 10–12, 2–5.
Closed Dec, Jan, 1–14 Oct
🖐 Inexpensive 🍴 Bar (€)
in Pirou

CHERBOURG

Ships have docked here since the 17th century when Vauban built the original port, and today a constant stream of ferries sail to and from England and Ireland. The art deco passenger terminal is now the **Cité de la Mer,** a celebration of seafaring heritage, with attractions including nuclear submarine *Le Redoutable*, a naval museum and a fabulous aquarium. The town has a life of its own, too, with theatre and restaurants grouped around the place Général de Gaulle, a pleasant pedestrianized shopping centre, and hotels and cafés overlooking the port and fishing boats. An eclectic collection in the Musée d'Ethnographie, set in tropical gardens, illustrates cultures and societies from around the world, including the Inuit (Eskimo). Above the town, Fort du Roule, the scene of fierce fighting in 1944, houses a museum about the war years.

In Tourlaville, 5km (3 miles) southeast of Cherbourg, the château (open all year) was the setting for a 16th-century sex scandal, when Julien and Marguerite Ravalet, children of the owners, ran off together and lived as lovers until they were convicted of incest and executed in 1603.

www.ot-cherbourg-cotentin.fr

✚ 2C 🍴 Choice of restaurants along quai de Caligny (€–€€)
🚌 From St-Lô 🚆 From Évreux and Caen (on line from Paris St-Lazare)

Cité de la Mer

✉ Gare Maritime Transatlantique ☎ 08 25 33 50 50 🕐 May–Jun, Sep daily 9:30–6; Jul, Aug daily 9:30–7; end Jan–Apr, Oct–Dec daily 10–6. Closed some Mons; ring for details

✋ Expensive

COUTANCES

The Gothic spires of the cathedral soar above the town on its outcrop overlooking the Soulles river. The present church, completed in 1274 with two graceful 80m (260ft) steeples and a 57m (187ft) octagonal lantern tower, replaced the Romanesque cathedral built by Bishop Geoffroy de Montbray in the mid-11th century. Inside, the eye is drawn upwards by the tall arcades, past lancet windows and stained glass to the vault, while light pours in through the side-chapel windows. The life of Thomas à Becket and the Day of Judgement are depicted in the magnificent transept windows.

Coutances is a peaceful and prosperous town, with public gardens laid out above the Bulsard tributary and the three remaining arches of its 14th-century aqueduct. The 17th-century Hôtel Poupinel at the garden's entrance houses the **Musée Quesnel-Morinière,** with paintings, furniture and dress.

www.ville-coutances.fr

✚ 2E 🍴 Choice of restaurants and cafés (€–€€) 🚌 From Cherbourg

Musée Quesnel-Morinière

✉ 2 rue Quesnel-Morinière ☎ 02 33 07 07 88 🕐 Jul–Aug Wed–Mon 11–6 (till 8 Thu); Sep–Jun Mon, Wed–Sat 10–12, 2–5, Sun 2–5. Closed Jan

✋ Inexpensive. Free Jul–Aug Thu 6–8, Sep–Jun Sun 2–5

GRANVILLE

Granville is a town with a many-sided character. There's the busy port with its lively fishing fleet, a terminal for ferries to the Channel Islands, and then there is the boisterous summer resort with shops, restaurants, and the modern Aquarium du Roc that houses a 'shell wonderland' and butterfly garden (➤ 69).

On the narrow headland above the modern town lies the Haute Ville, entered through a grim gateway (Grande Porte) complete with chained drawbridge. The upper town's ramparts were built by the English in the 15th century; within, houses huddle along the grid of streets that leads to the granite Église Notre-Dame and, behind it, the former barracks. Stone steps just inside the Grande Porte climb up to the **Musée du Vieux Granville,** which contains artefacts illustrating the history of the port.

Beyond the walls, the lighthouse on the Pointe du Roc offers good views; northeast, Christian Dior's childhood home has changing exhibits about the designer.

Boats travel to the nearby Îles Chausey, once quarried for granite. Just under 2km (1.2 miles) long, Grande Île is large enough for a small hotel, a 19th-century fort built against British attack, and a lighthouse.

www.ville-granville.fr

✚ 13H 🍴 Choice of restaurants on harbourside (€–€€€) 🚌 From Cherbourg 🚆 From Argentan (Paris Montparnasse line)

Musée du Vieux Granville

✉ 2 rue Le Carpentier ☎ 02 33 50 44 10 🕐 Apr–Sep Wed–Mon 10–12, 2–6 (till 6:30 in season); Oct–Mar Wed, Sat, Sun 2–6. Closed Jan ✋ Inexpensive

LESSAY

Lessay's abbey, Ste-Trinité, was founded in 1056 by Turstin Haldup, lord of la Haye-du-Puits, to the north, and completed early in the 12th century. The ancillary monastic buildings suffered in the Hundred Years and Religious wars, and, having been completely rebuilt in the 18th century, were destroyed in 1944. The restored church, however, survives as a fine example of Romanesque architecture, with glowing limestone walls and roof tiles covered in golden lichen. There are three tiers to the nave, with a gallery connecting the uppermost windows. Subdued stained glass adds to the simple tranquillity.

✚ 2E 🍴 Limited choice in town (€); or southeast on D900 and south on D57 to le Mesnilbus, Auberge des Bonnes Gens (€–€€€) 🚌 From Cherbourg

LE MONT-ST-MICHEL

Best places to see, pages 50–51.

MORTAIN

Mortain occupies a high ridge overlooking the steep Sélune Valley and Forêt de Mortain. The stark bell tower of Église St-Évroult rises above the main street; inside, the church treasury houses an 8th-century casket, the Chrismale, a reliquary decorated with angels and runic script, probably made in one of the English kingdoms. North of the centre, the buildings of the 12th-century **Abbaye Blanche** are actually dark and stern, despite the name. A walk from the abbey leads to two waterfalls – the Grande and Petite Cascade. **www.**ville-mortain.fr

🚌 15J 🍴 Bars and restaurants in town (€–€€)

Abbaye Blanche

☎ 02 33 79 47 47 🕐 Mid-Jun to Sep Wed–Sun 10–12, 2:30–6. Closed Sun am 🎫 Free

ST-LÔ

Following the bombardment of 1944 that destroyed most of its buildings St-Lô has been rebuilt as a modern town, but with a distinct character of its own. The old town walls survive in part and a single tower guards one corner of the central place Général-de-Gaulle. Market stalls set up under the roof of the tourist office; the office itself allows access to a modern tower giving views over the Vire Valley. The west front of the Église Notre-Dame has been left in its bomb-damaged state, the modern bronze doors a telling contrast to the battered 13th- to 17th-century façade; within,

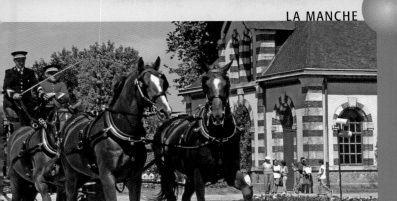

photographs show the extent of the wartime devastation. The
Musée des Beaux Arts in the Centre Culturel Jean Lurçat has
a collection of paintings and 16th-century tapestries.
www.saint-lo.fr

➕ 3E 🍴 Choice of restaurants and bars (€–€€) 🚌 From Cherbourg
🚆 From Caen

Musée des Beaux Arts
☎ 02 33 72 52 55 🕐 Wed–Mon 10–12, 2–6. Closed Jan–Mar

STE-MÈRE-ÉGLISE

In a modern building near the market place, the Musée des
Troupes Aéroportées commemorates the night of 5 June 1944
when paratroops were dropped over Ste-Mère-Église to support
the American army. Among them was Private John Steel, whose
parachute became entangled on the church steeple; he hung there
for two hours until captured by German soldiers. Each summer a
dummy parachutist is suspended from the steeple. A 16th-century
farm on the edge of town, the Ferme-Musée du Cotentin, has
displays about local rural life.
www.sainte-mere-eglise.info

➕ 3D 🍴 Some restaurants and cafés in town (€–€€) 🚌 From Cherbourg

ST-VAAST-LA-HOUGUE

Cafés overlook the harbour of this cheerful seaside town, famous for its oysters, where yachts and fishing boats jostle for space. Silhouetted at the tip of the southern causeway is Vauban's Fort de la Hougue. At the far end of a wharf is the Chapelle des Marins, a simple stone seamen's chapel with geometric carvings over the doorway. A bird sanctuary and the Musée Maritime of Tatihou Island lie across a narrow channel, a journey which can be made by boat or on foot when the tide is out (there's a limit to the number of visitors allowed per day).

www.saint-vaast-reville.com

🕂 3C 🍴 Choice of restaurants, especially near harbour (€–€€)

🚌 From Cherbourg

VALOGNES

The modern centre of Valognes, built after the war, is unremarkable, but the older quarter beyond has real charm. Mellow stone houses back on to a stream crossed by footbridges; one of them, the 15th-century Logis du Grand Quartier, houses the Musée Régional du Cidre et du Calvados, which tells the story of cider-making. Fragments of Roman buildings stand in a pleasant garden, and some grand 17th- to 18th-century houses survive, including the Hôtel Grandval-Caligny, home of 19th-century writer Jules Barbey d'Aurevilly, and the Hôtel de Beaumont, a graceful building with formal gardens.

www.mairie-valognes.fr

✠ 2C 🍴 Choice of hotel-restaurants in centre (€–€€€) 🚌 From Cherbourg
🚊 From Cherbourg (Paris St-Lazare line)

VILLEDIEU-LES-POÊLES

Copper pots and tin pans fill the shop windows of Villedieu's long main street (poêles means 'pans'). This has been a metalworking centre since the 12th century when the Knights Hospitallers (later 'of Malta') were established in the town. An alley leads from the main street between dark granite houses to the Maison de l'Étain (House of Pewter), while opposite is the Atelier du Cuivre (copper workshop). Bells are still cast in the **Fonderie de Cloches,** set on an island in the Sienne. There are yet more attractions crowded into the little town: a lace-making museum; a clockmaker's workshop; and the Musée du Meuble Normand, across the Sienne behind the main street, with its traditional Norman furniture.

www.ot-villedieu.fr

✠ 15H 🍴 Restaurants, bars (€–€€) 🚊 From Granville/ Argentan/Vire (Paris Montparnasse line)

Fonderie de Cloches

✉ Atelier Cornille Harvard, 10 rue du Pont Chignon ☎ 02 33 61 00 56
🕓 7 Feb–11 Nov Tue–Sat 10–12:30, 2–5:30; Jul, Aug daily 9–6
✋ Inexpensive

a drive through the Vallée de la Vire

This route winds up and down the green Vire Valley, through peaceful *bocage* countryside.

Take the N174 from St-Lô (➤ 176) to Torigni-sur-Vire.

This fast road sweeps through wooded, rolling farmland to Torigni, a small town with a camping site and lakes, where the Château des Matignon has a display of 17th- and 18th-century tapestries and sculptures.

At the junction by the château, turn right (Tessy-sur-Vire). Cross the roundabout and turn right just before the water tower; then follow signs left, through Brectouville, and right to Roches de Ham.

The road climbs gradually past farms and orchards to this spectacular 80m (262ft) viewpoint looking down over the curving river and its valley.

Return down the D551 to a right turn (D396), crossing the Vire and climbing the other side of the valley. Turn left to Troisgots and la-Chapelle-sur-Vire.

Pilgrims still come to la Chapelle's riverside church to see its 15th-century statue of Our Lady of Vire. On the opposite bank an ornate gateway and steps lead to the Stations of the Cross.

Turn left with the D159/D359, crossing the river again. At a junction, turn right to Tessy-sur-Vire. Then take the D374/D21 (signed Vire) through Pont-Farcy, and turn left (D307) to Ste-Marie-Outre-l'Eau. The road swings

left round the church. Follow the D307 past the Pont-Bellenger turning for the D185 to Campeaux. Join the N174 (right, to Vire), then turn left (D293) and follow the river to the D56 (right) and le Bény-Bocage.

There are good views of the upper Vire Valley from this attractive town, and several good viewpoints near by.

After leaving le Bény-Bocage turn right (D577) and continue to Vire (▶ 156).

Distance 75km (47 miles)

Time About 2.5 hours, without stops

Start point St-Lô
🚩 3E

End point Vire
🚩 16H

Lunch Auberge de la Chapelle (€)
✉ Troisgots, north of la-Chapelle-sur-Vire ☎ 02 33 56 32 83

HOTELS

BARNEVILLE-CARTERET
Hôtel de la Marine (€€–€€€)
Cheerful hotel overlooking the sea and port. Expensive rooms; terrace with tables in summer. Parking and an excellent restaurant.
✉ 11 rue de Paris ☎ 02 33 53 83 31 🕐 Closed 3 Nov–19 Feb

CHERBOURG
Ambassadeur Hôtel (€–€€)
Bright, well-designed rooms, double-glazed against the busy port near by. Parking behind the hotel.
✉ 22 quai de Caligny ☎ 02 33 43 10 00 🕐 Closed late Dec

Hôtel Mercure (€€–€€€)
Modern building, strangely isolated beside the port. Convenient for the car ferry, but less so for the town centre and restaurants.
✉ Allée Président Menut ☎ 02 33 44 01 11

Hôtel la Régence (€–€€)
Pleasant Logis de France hotel in a white quayside building, with simply furnished rooms, parking at the rear, and a brasserie-style restaurant.
✉ 42 quai de Caligny ☎ 02 33 43 05 16 🕐 Closed 24 Dec–2 Jan

COUTANCES
Hôtel le Normandie (€)
Small hotel behind the cathedral, with a restaurant (closed Mon in winter, Sun eve) serving good-value meals. Parking.
✉ 2 place Général-de-Gaulle ☎ 02 33 45 01 40

GRANVILLE
Hôtel le Grand Large (€–€€€)
See page 75.

LE MONT-ST-MICHEL
Hôtel la Croix Blanche (€€–€€€)
See page 75.

Hôtel du Mouton Blanc (€€)
Attractive stone and timber building, with a good restaurant and sea views. The cheapest rooms – by the standards of le Mont-St-Michel – are very reasonable.

✉ Grande rue ☎ 02 33 60 14 08

VILLEDIEU-LES-POÊLES
Hôtel le Fruitier (€–€€)
See page 75.

See page 75.

RESTAURANTS

BARFLEUR
Hôtel Moderne (€–€€€)
Restaurant-with-rooms serving salmon dishes, oysters and goat's cheese *millefeuille*. Cheaper set menu during the week.

✉ 1 place de Gaulle ☎ 02 33 23 12 44 🕐 Lunch, dinner. Closed mid-Jan to mid-Mar, Wed mid-Sep to mid-Jan, Tue Sep–Jun

BARNEVILLE-CARTERET
Hôtel de la Marine (€€–€€€)
Pricey but stylish hotel-restaurant; oysters with innovative sauces, salmon and a delicious dark chocolate tart.

✉ 11 rue de Paris ☎ 02 33 53 83 31 🕐 Lunch, dinner. Closed end Nov–early Mar

CHERBOURG
Café de Paris (€–€€)
Live lobsters in tanks; good range of seafood dishes and a good-value set menu in this café overlooking the port.

✉ 40 quai de Caligny ☎ 02 33 43 12 36 🕐 Lunch, dinner. Closed early Nov

Le Grandgousier (€–€€€)
Stylish but friendly service. Classy touches to a wide range of seafood options, including caviar, crab claws, shellfish and salmon.

✉ 21 rue de l'Abbaye ☎ 02 33 53 19 43 🕐 Lunch, dinner. Closed Mon

La Régence (€€)
See page 59.

GRANVILLE
Citadelle (€–€€)
Splendid views across the harbour from this popular eatery with a covered terrace. Seafood and hearty Norman country fare.
✉ 34 rue du Port ☎ 02 33 50 34 10 🕐 Lunch, dinner. Closed Wed, and Tue Oct–Mar

Horizon (€–€€)
The restaurant at the Hotel des Bains is as classy as one would expect of a resort dining room, yet menus range from budget value to adventurous seafood treats.
✉ Place Maréchal Foch ☎ 02 33 50 00 79 🕐 Lunch, dinner

LE MONT-ST-MICHEL
Hôtel la Croix Blanche (€–€€)
A well-placed hotel-restaurant with good food at reasonable prices, and tasty omelettes to compete with the famous Poulard version (see below).
✉ Grande Rue ☎ 02 33 60 14 03 🕐 Lunch, dinner. Closed mid-Nov to mid-Feb

La Mère Poulard (€€–€€€)
Famous hotel-restaurant, with renowned omelettes made to the recipe devised by Madame Poulard in the late 19th century. Fine bay views.
✉ Grande Rue ☎ 02 33 89 68 68 🕐 Lunch, dinner

ST-VAAST-LA-HOUGUE
Les Fuschias (€€)
One of the most popular Logis restaurants in Normandy. Home cooking with a professional flair. A veranda opens on to the private garden.
✉ 20 rue Maréchal Foch ☎ 02 33 54 42 26 🕐 Lunch, dinner. Closed Tue eve Nov–Mar, Mon, Tue lunch except Jul, Aug

Index

SHOPPING

FASHION
Gulliver

Smart leather footwear for children, including a range of multi-coloured suede shoes.

✉ 4 rue des Fossés, Cherbourg ☎ 02 33 53 83 83

FOOD
Maison Gosselin

One of the finest grocer's shops in the region. From the delicatessen counters serving cheeses and meats to the excellent wine cellars and an enviable range of calvados and whiskies, this family business is marked by a love of fine food and drink.

✉ Rue de Verrüe, St-Vaast-la-Hougue ☎ 02 33 54 40 06

GIFTS
A Cosnefroy

Textiles, umbrellas, lamps, dolls; all kinds of everything in a cluttered but welcoming little shop.

✉ 18 rue au Blé, Cherbourg ☎ 02 33 93 19 27

ENTERTAINMENT

LIVE MUSIC
Casino Cherbourg

Disco, pub and restaurant on the quayside.

✉ 18 quai Alexandre III, Cherbourg ☎ 02 33 43 00 56

THEATRE AND CONCERT HALLS
Archipel

Good, varied programme at this showcase theatre in the resort.

✉ Place Maréchal Foch, Granville ☎ 02 33 69 27 30

Théâtre de Cherbourg

Set in an ornate building with a good café-restaurant attached; visiting orchestras, dance troupes and drama companies are included in a lively programme.

✉ Place Général-de-Gaulle, Cherbourg ☎ 02 33 88 55 55

Acknowledgements

The Automobile Association would like to thank the following photographers, companies and picture libraries for their assistance in the preparation of this book.

Abbreviations for the picture credits are as follows – (t) top; (b) bottom; (c) centre; (l) left; (r) right; (AA) AA World Travel Library.

4l St-Vaast-la-Hougue AA/C Sawyer; **4c** Cherbourg AA/R Moore; **4r** Château Gaillard AA/C Sawyer; **5l** Barneville-Carteret AA/I Dawson; **5c** Monet's house AA/C Sawyer; **6/7** St-Vaast-la-Hougue AA/C Sawyer; **8/9** Boulangerie AA/C Sawyer; **10cr** Sign © CDT Calvados; **10bl** Grocer's © CDT Calvados; **10br** Château de Vendeuvre © Vudoiseau; **10/11** Pont de Normandie © Dieter Basse; **11cl** Local drinks © J F Lefevre; **11cr** Apple blossom © J F Lefevre; **11bl** Apples AA/R Moore; **12cr** Cheese AA/I Dawson; **12b** Cheeses AA/R Moore; **12/13** Cheese display AA/C Sawyer; **13cl** Oysters © G Wait; **13b** Mussels AA/R Moore; **14t** Boudin noir AA/R Moore; **14b** Cider bottles AA/I Dawson; **15tl** Calvados AA/R Moore; **15cl** Cider barrel AA/I Dawson; **15r** Apples AA/R Moore; **15bl** Tarte normande AA/R Moore; **16bl** Oysters AA/R Moore; **16br** Lyons Forest AA/R Moore; **16/17** Mont-St-Michel © H P Reiser; **17** Brecy Calvados © Vudoiseau; **18/19** Goury © Dieter Basse; **19t** Horse riding © CRT Calvados; **19b** Farmhouse cider AA/I Dawson; **20/21** Cherbourg AA/R Moore; **24** Fireworks AA/M Lynch; **26** Toll AA/J A Tims; **27** Ferry AA/I Dawson; **28** Bus AA/P Bennett; **31** Telephone AA/P Bennett; **34/35** Château Gaillard AA/C Sawyer; **36** Abbaye de Jumièges AA/I Dawson; **37t** Window AA/M Moss; **37b** Arches AA/M Moss; **38** Castle AA/C Sawyer; **38/39** Les Andelys AA/C Sawyer; **40** Bayeux tapestry © Goélette Tapisserie de Bayeux; **40/41** Detail © Tapisserie de Bayeux; **42/43t** Interior AA/R Moore; **42/43b** Château d'O AA/C Sawyer; **44/45** Market AA/P Bennett; **45** Port AA/C Sawyer; **46t** Shop sign AA/C Sawyer; **46b** Fishing boats AA/I Dawson; **46/47** Café AA/C Sawyer; **48** Memorial sign AA/B Smith; **49** Exhibition AA/C Sawyer; **48/49** Flags AA/I Dawson; **50** Refectory AA/C Sawyer; **50/51** Mont-St-Michel AA/C Sawyer; **52/53** Interior © Florian Kleinnefenn collection SENN, Musée Malraux; **53** On the beach, 1863 (w/c & pastel on paper) Eugène Boudin (1824–98), Musée Marmottan, Paris, Giraudon/The Bridgeman Art Library; **54cl** Coat of arms AA/R Moore; **54br** Clock detail © B Voisin - OT de Rouen; **55** Gros Horloge AA/C Sawyer; **56/57** Barneville-Carteret AA/I Dawson; **58** Restaurant © Dormy House; **60/61** Horse riding AA/I Dawson; **62/63** Perseigne forest AA/R Moore; **64/65** Camembert AA/R Moore; **67** Étretat AA/R Moore; **68/69** Canoeing AA/P Bennett; **70/71** Château Gaillard © Dieter Basse; **72** Golf AA/S Day; **74/75** Hotel © Château les Bruyères; **76/77** Monet's house AA/C Sawyer; **79** Le Tréport AA/P Bennett; **80** Old houses © B Voisin - OT de Rouen; **81** Stained glass © SL-Convergencephotos.com; **82** Cathedral AA/R Moore; **83** Richard the Lionheart's tomb AA/R Moore; **84** Église St-Maclou AA/R Moore; **85** Ceramics museum AA/R Moore; **86/87t** Detail AA/I Dawson; **86/87b** Palais de Justice AA/I Dawson; **88** Statue AA/I Dawson; **88/89** Timber-framed houses AA/R Moore; **90/91** Monks AA/R Moore; **91** Arques-la-Bataille AA/C Sawyer; **92** Église St-Nicolas AA/P Bennett; **95l** Entrance gate AA/C Sawyer; **95r** Château d'Anet AA/C Sawyer; **96/97** Château de Beaumesnil AA/P Bennett; **98** Château de Miromesnil © Vudoiseau; **99** Wallaby AA/R Moore; **100/101t** Ecouis AA/P Bennett; **100/101b** Étretat AA/I Dawson; **102/103** Yport AA/C Sawyer; **104/105** Forest of Eu AA/C Sawyer; **105** Fountain AA/C Sawyer; **106t** Copper stills AA/C Sawyer; **106/107b** Monet's garden AA/C Sawyer; **108** Lighthouse AA/I Dawson; **108/109** Lyons-la-Forêt AA/C Sawyer; **110** Market AA/R Moore; **113** Varengeville-sur-Mer AA/R Moore; **114** Église de la Madeleine AA/C Sawyer; **115** Verneuil-sur-Avre AA/C Sawyer; **125** Ouistreham AA/C Sawyer; **126** Abbaye aux Dames AA/I Dawson; **126/127** Abbaye aux Hommes AA/I Dawson; **128** Timber-framed buildings AA/R Moore; **129t** Rue St-Pierre AA/R Moore; **129b** Abbaye aux Hommes © CDT Calvados; **130** Château AA/R Moore; **131** Église St-Pierre AA/R Moore; **132** Tower AA/C Sawyer; **132/133** Mulberry harbour AA/I Dawson; **134** War cemetery AA/I Dawson; **135** Beuvron-en-Auge AA/R Moore; **136/137** Cabourg AA/R Moore; **138** Château de Carrouges AA/C Sawyer; **139** Château de Fontaine-Henry AA/R Moore; **140/141** Château de Vendeuvre AA/P Bennett; **141** River Orne AA/C Sawyer; **142/143** Racecourse AA/R Moore; **143** Domfront AA/P Bennett; **144/145** William the Conqueror statue AA/R Moore; **145** Le Haras du Pin AA/R Moore; **146** Sainte Thérèse AA/R Moore; **147** Postcards AA/R Moore; **148** Ouistreham © CDT Calvados; **150/151** Juno Beach © CDT Calvados; **151** Arromanches © CDT Calvados; **152** Roche d'Oêtre AA/C Sawyer; **152/153** Château St-Germain-de-Livet AA/P Bennett; **154** Thury-Harcourt gardens AA/C Sawyer; **154/155** Beach huts AA/R Moore; **155** Trouville AA/C Sawyer; **156t** Vire © Phil Portus/Alamy; **156b** Andouille AA/R Moore; **165** Cherbourg AA/R Moore; **166/167** Abbaye de Lucerne AA/I Dawson; **167** Manuscripts © Scriptorial d'Avranches; **168/169t** Château AA/R Moore; **168/169c** Lobster pots AA/I Dawson; **170** Cérisy-la-Forêt © Dieter Basse; **171** Château de Pirou AA/P Bennett; **172** Cherbourg AA/C Sawyer; **173** Coutances AA/C Sawyer; **174/175** Granville AA/I Dawson; **175** Lessay AA/C Sawyer; **176** Abbaye Blanche, Mortain AA/R Moore; **176/177** St-Lô stud farm © Dieter Basse; **178** St-Vaast-la-Hougue AA/C Sawyer; **180/181** Vire–Roches-du-Ham © Dieter Basse

Every effort has been made to trace the copyright holders, and we apologise in advance for any accidental errors. We would be happy to apply the corrections in the following edition of this publication.

Sight Locator Index

This index relates to the maps on the cover. We have given map references to the main sights in the book. Some sights within towns may not be plotted on the maps.

Dear Reader

Your comments, opinions and recommendations are very important to us. Please help us to improve our travel guides by taking a few minutes to complete this simple questionnaire.

You do not need a stamp (unless posted outside the UK). If you do not want to cut this page from your guide, then photocopy it or write your answers on a plain sheet of paper.

Send to: **The Editor, AA World Travel Guides, FREEPOST SCE 4598, Basingstoke RG21 4GY.**

Your recommendations...

We always encourage readers' recommendations for restaurants, nightlife or shopping – if your recommendation is used in the next edition of the guide, we will send you a **FREE AA Guide** of your choice from this series. Please state below the establishment name, location and your reasons for recommending it.

_____

_____

_____

_____

_____

Please send me **AA Guide** _____

About this guide...

Which title did you buy?

    AA _____

Where did you buy it? _____

When? m m / y y

Why did you choose this guide? _____

_____

_____

_____

_____

Did this guide meet your expectations?

Exceeded ☐   Met all ☐   Met most ☐   Fell below ☐

Were there any aspects of this guide that you particularly liked? _____

_____

_____

_____

continued on next page...

Is there anything we could have done better? _____

_____

_____

_____

About you...
Name (Mr/Mrs/Ms) _____

Address _____

_____

_____ Postcode _____

Daytime tel nos _____

Email _____

Please only give us your mobile phone number or email if you wish to hear from us about other products and services from the AA and partners by text or mms, or email.

Which age group are you in?
Under 25 ☐   25–34 ☐   35–44 ☐   45–54 ☐   55–64 ☐   65+ ☐

How many trips do you make a year?
Less than one ☐   One ☐   Two ☐   Three or more ☐

Are you an AA member? Yes ☐   No ☐

About your trip...
When did you book? m m / y y   When did you travel? m m / y y

How long did you stay? _____

Was it for business or leisure? _____

Did you buy any other travel guides for your trip? _____

If yes, which ones? _____

_____

_____

Thank you for taking the time to complete this questionnaire. Please send it to us as soon as possible, and remember, you do not need a stamp (unless posted outside the UK).

| **AA** Travel Insurance call 0800 072 4168 or visit www.theAA.com |